TAROT THERAPY

TAROT THERAPY

A NEW APPROACH TO SELF EXPLORATION

JAN WOUDHUYSEN

FOREWORD BY EILEEN CONNOLLY

JEREMY P. TARCHER, INC.
Los Angeles
Distributed by St. Martin's Press
New York

Library of Congress Cataloging in Publication Data

Woudhuysen, Jan.
   [Tarotmania]
   Tarot therapy: a new approach to self exploration / Jan Woudhuysen; foreword
by Eileen Connolly.
      p.   cm.
   Originally published under title: Tarotmania.
   Reprint. Originally published: Los Angeles: J.P. Tarcher, 1980, c1979.
   ISBN 0-87477-470-5
   1. Tarot.   I. Title.
BF1879.T2W6 1988
133.3'2424—dc19   88-1850
                                                    CIP

Jeremy P. Tarcher, Inc.
9110 Sunset Blvd.
Los Angeles, CA 90069

Manufactured in the United States of America
10   9   8   7   6   5   4   3   2

First published in Great Britain 1979

To my Mother
Who always let me walk alone,
and caught me when I fell

CONTENTS

THE PROMISE
I'll give you air
Water and earth
And flame from a gentle sun
Till in your heart
The flower unfolds
Towards the warm light
Simply, unknowingly
Instinctive but right

FOREWORD

Jan Woudhuysen takes a unique and seemingly lighthearted approach to the ancient esoteric science of Tarot. His approach is yet another way to see what the Tarot has to offer. This book would make an excellent companion for travelers waiting at the airport or railway station. It lets the reader step right into the wisdom of Tarot and encourages him to become involved without commitment. After the reader has completed his journey, he will probably do one of two things: close the book and come back to it later, or research Tarot further and become an avid Tarotologist.

I'm sure the reader will be as much aware of the author as he is of the book, for Woudhuysen's personality is dominant throughout. He has many stories to tell and is quite persuasive. I must say that as it is presented in this work, the process of learning appears comparatively easy. The knowledge of symbology found in Tarot cards is not to be considered a deterrent, and the accepted forms of interpretation are not a prerequisite. These ideas could be an irresistible invitation to divination for the new Tarot student.

Woudhuysen explains in some detail that "the Major Arcana is a much deeper psychologically or mystically oriented series, whereas the Minor Arcana is more about the everyday events that occur." I took a stroll through his personal garden of Major Arcana and realized his Gardener was his Magician. His clever and somewhat cynical description of the Arcanas is a personal one and is unfamiliar to me. However, a tongue-in-cheek response from the reader may match the possible intent of the author. When I entered his Vegetable Garden I did so with a grain of salt.

I also took a good look into the author's Psychic Mirror and saw a well-defined image of the three levels of consciousness. If the reader feels he is limited due to his lack of psychic ability, he can use this knowledge to alleviate such self-doubts, which may inevitably spur him to become a Tarot enthusiast. Although Woudhuysen does not disbelieve in the mystical approach, he describes how one can use Tarot without concern over whether one has a natural aptitude for it. This original approach is very appealing and may encourage many to study this ancient art without feeling compelled to take it too seriously.

Woudhuysen touches on esoteric philosophies and presents interesting challenges regarding the use and interpretation of Tarot symbology. We are told to use Tarot as ''a rough and ready, but especially quick means to understanding other people, in a professional way.'' This is one of the major keys to his work. The intricacies of Tarotology are not considered; therefore, we are free to explore and follow his warm and humorous guidance. We are not confronted with Tarot's heights and depths; instead, the author leads us into the pastures of our own opinion, providing guidelines for individual personal adventure. The book also contains linear spreads, along with spreads of decision and choice, plus a touch of the Cabala. Woudhuysen encourages the reader to design his own spreads and describes several methods.

There is a sense of freedom throughout *Tarot Therapy*. It does not lock the reader into any preconceived ideas. There is no sense of restriction or form; consequently, I see the book as a universal passport into the world of esoteric thought. I might add that the visa issued is probably limited.

I like Woudhuysen's brief but precise distinctions between the esoteric and the exoteric. Keeping in mind the awakening of the New Age, I would venture to say that more works of this exoteric nature could bring the student to the realms of esoteric possibility. Therefore I find *Tarot Therapy* provocative and challenging. It represents a view of the esoteric that gives the reader *carte blanche* by allowing an unusual access to the exciting world of Tarot.

The end result of this reading experience should be one of mental challenge or enjoyment, depending on how far the reader has traveled on the Royal Road of Tarot. In the exoteric and esoteric journey of life, there is always room for a companion such as Jan Woudhuysen.

—EILEEN CONNOLLY

part one

Chapter 1

TAROT IN A MODERN SETTING

This book is intended to be totally unlike all other books on the Tarot. Most books work on the assumption that there is a definitive meaning of the Tarot to be found somewhere; if the book is honest it will add that the meanings given in the book are the generally accepted ones, but it will still have been written on the assumption that somewhere are to be found the *real* meanings. Perhaps the real meanings are in the possession of a small esoteric group, hidden from the general public; perhaps the real meanings are lost in time. But somewhere they exist, or have existed, and once they are found, then any reasonably intelligent person can use the cards to find out everything. The few books that don't assume this, merely omit to tell you that fact; the author simply tells you what the meanings are, usually by the aid of a special system derived from, say, the Egyptians.

This book is an attempt to set down in writing a series of lectures, discussions, demonstrations and games which were conducted for the purpose of teaching ordinary people what the Tarot can be about. As I will explain later in the book, the study of the Tarot and the struggle to understand it is in fact a method of self-development of the psyche. Such a development cannot take place without objective guidance from an outside teacher, in the same way that Freudian analysis cannot be undertaken except by someone who has been analysed in the past. The actual meaning of the cards is not very important, nor are the spreads in which they are used (spreads are the patterns in which the cards are laid out during a reading). The important things are the way in which the meanings are obtained, and the manner in which the cards are used. The problem then arises that it is easy to set out the meanings of the cards, and the

pattern of the spreads, whereas it is much more difficult to set out
learning methods which are applicable to each individual in turn. It
is easier to present facts than to change people's behaviour or
thoughts. Nonetheless, however difficult, I shall try just this once.

I will go a little further into why it is difficult to write a book which
will teach the use of Tarot. When we have to learn facts, these facts
may be set out on paper in the form of a list, numbered, and with an
illustration of the purpose to which each fact can be put. The list is
memorized, the exam is taken, and that is that. But when we try to
change someone's behaviour, we need to arrange for 'feed-back'
from the pupil to the teacher. When the pupil shows signs of having
misunderstood the matter being taught, the teacher rephrases it till
the pupil *does* understand. It is also important that the teacher can
see whether the pupil has reached that stage in his development at
which the material can be taken in. The situation of the pupil will
restrict the type and amount of information he can absorb; the
teacher has to allow for this, and so on. Teaching the use of the
Tarot is not a matter of setting out facts, but is in essence a way of
getting people to look at the facts they already know, and in a
different way.

I therefore have to imagine all the different people who will come
across this book, in all their different stages of development, and
write down my ideas so that they will apply to all. So you, the reader,
will read this book at a time when it may be of very little relevance;
you may understand it very differently from what I intended. Bear
this in mind when you read it; if it doesn't work for you, or you get
impatient, put it aside and return to it in a few years time, or when
you are feeling in a different mood. Just don't push matters.

* * *

Tarot cards and fortune-telling have been associated for many
centuries. When we think of the Tarot, we think of Gypsies or
strange gentlemen in clothing decorated with mystic symbols.
Books mention it as part of the plot, or describe it as part of the
colourful background of fairs and circuses. Most of us, at some time
or other, have seen a sign offering us the opportunity of learning
about our future; usually when we go in there is an old lady who

grabs our palm, looks at us closely, and starts muttering about a dark gentleman who is to cross our path, or a journey across the water, perhaps a fortune waiting for us. We think of fortune-telling as a way of predicting events that will come to pass in the future.

But the same event may happen to two different people, and mean something totally different. A tall dark handsome stranger crossing the path of a respectably married lady is different, to an alarming degree, from the same prediction applied to a young girl of sixteen. Similarly, the same event could happen to the same people at different times in their lives to produce totally different reactions:

> When the doctor had finished his examination, he smiled and remarked, 'Mrs. Smith, I have some good news for you.' Upon her responding that she was a Miss, and not a Mrs., he changed that to: 'Miss Smith, I have some bad news for you.'

We can say that the exoteric use of the Tarot is to foretell *what* will happen to the Querent, but the esoteric way is to predict what it will *mean* to him. The meaning it has for the Querent also allows us to predict how he will react to events, and what his feelings will be.

The Tarot certainly can be used for predicting the future. Its accuracy will depend on how accurately and objectively we see the present and the past; if we knew the complete past down to every tiny detail, and all the facts and feelings of the present, then we could predict the future with complete accuracy. For instance, we see a child holding a large ball on the ground at the top of a hill; the child lets go of the ball, and we can predict that it will fall down to the foot of the hill. Real problems in the world which cause worry to real people are usually much more complicated, and so we are tempted to say that we cannot see the whole situation, and hence we cannot predict. But, in fact the picture of the boy holding the ball on top of the hill is incomplete. We have ignored the colour of the sky, the day of the week, and the type of clothes the boy is wearing. They are not pertinent to the problem, and we have left them out for that reason. In the same way, if we take only those facts which are relevant to the problem, then the whole problem becomes much simpler to solve.

Tarot provides a way of selecting only the facts which have a bearing on the problem. The decision as to which facts are relevant, and which can be ignored, is taken at a level beyond our conscious control; we have no access to this point in ourselves and are, in fact, unaware of the process. When we ask a question through the Tarot, this mystic part of us will release the answer, but it will not tell us how it arrived at this answer. The rationalist will therefore reject the answer, rather like a school teacher who will not accept the result of a sum, however correct, unless the pupil can show how he got there. But in the real life of our everyday experiences we know that very often obtaining good results using a rule of thumb method is better than totally correct results obtained through correct academic usage.

A good example is to be found when learning a foreign language. I spent six years learning French, often two or three hours a week making a total of 600 hours or four months. At the end of this I could hardly write enough correct French to pass an exam, and I certainly couldn't write a letter to anybody. We were given vocabularies to learn, the declensions of verbs, grammatical procedure; all our translated sentences were marked, with one point lost for each mistake. Accuracy, total faultless academic accuracy, was all. About my fourth year or so, a French visitor came to stay with my parents who very kindly relieved me of some of the pressure caused by too much homework. I copied her French exercises accurately in my own fair hand, only to receive them back from the teacher with far more mistakes annotated than I ever made. Also, about this time I discovered that although I was translating uninteresting stories about the Family Dubois, and still getting very mediocre marks, I could read a French newspaper, and understand most of it. Gradually it dawned on me that the very precision demanded at school was in fact *preventing* me from learning to speak and understand French.

The best way to learn French is to use it, however badly and clumsily. The more you use it, the more often you have a chance to pick up correct usage through osmosis, the way children learn to speak a language. Eventually you will get to be accurate 95% of the time without ever quite knowing how that came about. The area beyond our control knows the rules and tells the hand or mouth the correct decisions. If you don't believe that, look at the word 'ambiguity' and repeat it perhaps thirty or forty times, trying to vary the pronunciation. Now try to write it down. The same applies to any word which we make a conscious effort to spell correctly. In practice, most people just allow their hands to write it down without looking at the spelling; only when it looks wrong do they check.

The Tarot produces results in a similar way. How these are produced should not concern our conscious minds. We can, however, train our conscious mind to make better use of the work done by the mystic part of ourselves, and that is the purpose of training in the Tarot.

* * *

There is in fact much more to the Tarot. In ordinary fortune-telling we use the cards to give us an answer about the future. The esoteric system (I will explain later what 'esoteric' means) allows us to use the cards to answer many other types of question, and what is more, to suggest new ones. The ability to make use of the inherent powers of intuition is the reward given to those using the system; the ability to generate new questions the unique attribute. The Tarot can be used to help you come to terms with yourself, or to understand other people. If we can understand ourselves better, we have an opportunity to grow. If we understand other people better, we can build up better relationships.

The Tarot is a means of linking our conscious and our subconscious. The subconscious which knows and perceives all, and the conscious which is bewildered by events. We all have the gift of intuition, but most of us suppress it. This book will attempt to educate the conscious into giving the subconscious permission to do its work without hindrance. If you approach what is written with an open and receptive attitude, are prepared to do the work and exercises suggested, and are willing to consider new ideas, then there is no reason why you should not be able to use the Tarot cards.

The Tarot has always been used for 'fortune-telling' although in fact many traditional practitioners have used it for purposes which nowadays would be called psychotherapeutic. My purpose in setting up the lectures in the first place was to try to attract the attention of those professionally interested in the various forms of psychotherapy in the use of the Tarot.

The Tarot permits very quick 'fits' of character and problem analysis at considerable depth. By this I mean that we can obtain 95% accuracy at the first stab, rather in the way that most men can be fitted immediately with ready-to-wear clothes; it is only the occasional man who needs to have clothes especially tailored for him because his body size or proportions are so exceptional. Having clothes especially tailored takes time and is very expensive, and the difference between a good ready-to-wear and a cheap made-to-measure is very small. In everyday life we accept the cheaper alternative as perfectly reasonable. Similarly, there is no reason why the Tarot shouldn't be used in the vast majority of cases to arrive at insights which are correct for all ordinary purposes, rather than spend six months or a year to arrive at only marginally better ones.

Another analogy would be to compare the ease by which we can multiply the two numbers 56 and 79, and then divide by 26 if we use paper and pencil, or if we do it in our heads. First find paper and pencil, then multiply correctly, and lastly divide to get an accurate 170. But in our heads we say that 56×79 is almost the same as 55×80, or 110×40, which is obviously 4,400. 4,400 divided by 26 is almost the same as 4,400 divided by 25, and since the first number is a bit over, let the division be a little under. 4,400 divided by 25 is equal to 8,800 by 50 or 17,600 by 100, and that comes to 176. It looks complicated when set out on paper, but goes much more quickly in your head, and it is only 3% wrong. And don't tell me about pocket calculators; the type of mental calculations I have described above I do routinely so as to check that I haven't pressed a wrong button somewhere, or that the fragile temperamental thing hasn't missed an electron.

So, in a similar way, I am proposing the use of the Tarot as a rough and ready, but especially *quick* means to understanding other people in the professional way. Psychotherapy often takes a long term view; a proper psychoanalysis will take many years, and even everyday 'cosmetic' therapy may take six months or a year to get somewhere. This may not sound long, but often a patient or client comes when things are near a crisis, or have reached a climax; when a child or wife is being battered, a marriage breaking down, or a disturbed patient is bringing up very young and impressionable children, then by the time some results are reached in conventional therapy the damage to other people interacting with the patient may already have been done.

Lastly, the Tarot not only detects the problem in many cases, it also suggests the remedy in a way that is suitable to the particular person and their particular problem. This aspect of the Tarot is especially useful, since most psychotherapy takes the time not in finding the problem as far as the therapist is concerned, but in training the patient to see it him- or herself.

* * *

All religions and most forms of learning have an esoteric and an exoteric side. You will have seen the word esoteric many times during the last few years, and probably associate it with words like magic, mystic, mysterious, etc. It actually has a very precise meaning; it is used to denote those parts of any body of knowledge which are to be told only to the initiated. The exoteric part of the religion can be told to everyone, but only if they promise to keep it secret will any person be told the esoteric part.

Obviously, this immediately raises the next question, which is why did certain parts have to be kept secret in the first place. The first possibility may be that the priests have an outlook on many matters which is in violent disagreement with the view held by the population as a whole, or perhaps just the ruling part. Often, the priest is better educated, more in touch with modern ideas, and may have liberal attitudes towards controversial ideas which would cause him to be killed or at least punished if they became generally known. That is the historical reason. But another reason is that many ideas can become powerful tools for people who understand them, but will be destructive or malign if presented to people who are not yet ready for them. A proper grasp of business practice and attitudes can be of great use to a grown man, but would be sad and perhaps a little unhealthy in a six-year-old boy. I have known very young children who went daily through their stamp collection reckoning up its value with the aid of a catalogue, and swapping these stamps with unsuspecting possessors of rare stamps. Similarly, while sex education may be thought necessary and even beneficial to young children, there is no need to discuss the sexual perversions of mentally disturbed adults mentioned in heavy medical tomes. All knowledge must come when the person acquiring it is prepared and can understand it in its context.

Originally this meant that a great part of any religion could be written about and discussed by anyone; if you felt that it appealed to you strongly, you might join the religion, and after a suitable period of training and probation you would be judged ready for initiation. At a special ceremony you would take an oath to keep the esoteric information secret, and then you would be told all that was felt to be suitable at that stage. Often there were a number of stages, and the initiate would ascend each in turn, till he reached the innermost sanctum. Because it was to be kept secret, it is difficult to know and find out about historical forms of esoteric knowledge; hence the association the word has with mysterious, magic, etc.

This book does not promise to provide esoteric knowledge of the Tarot, since to the best of my knowledge there is no secret religion or society of Tarot which readers can join if they are judged worthy to receive further knowledge. There is however a modern way of looking at the division between esoteric and exoteric, and this book will try to discuss the second way of looking at this difference.

If you have ever tried to explain how a motor car works to a three-year-old boy, you will come up against the fact that the things you as an adult know are extremely difficult to explain to someone who doesn't have a whole lot of facts at his fingertips. In fact, the three-year-old might not even want to know. James Thurber quotes a little girl returning a book about penguins to the library and complaining that the book in question had told her far more about penguins than she wished to know. Similarly, the little boy only wants to know that you press this button, turn that wheel, and that the pedal on the right makes the car go faster; many adults who are totally dependent on their car still wish to know only that. The knowledge of how to use the car might be likened to the exoteric, whilst the esoteric knowledge is made up of facts about gas-flow diagrams, circuits, and gear-wheel ratios. Most people are supremely indifferent to these facts; the knowledge is there for all to read in the libraries, but most people just cannot be bothered. Yet when the car goes wrong, they take it to a garage to get it fixed, since they don't understand all the technical bits. At the garage there are people who *do* understand cars; you might say they have esoteric knowledge. And it is in this sense that I can say that this book will provide esoteric knowledge; it contains facts and ideas that are available to anyone, but that not everyone would have the time and patience to gather and sift.

Although I have gathered facts and ideas which can be used by you to study, the actual pursuit will still demand a great deal of work from you. Not the work of memorizing, but the work involved in understanding parts of yourself, and changing your attitudes and preconceptions.

Chapter 2

TAROT AND ITS LACK OF HISTORY

People often ask where it all began. They ask, what is its history, how did it develop, who invented it.

Before I go on any further, I must explain what is meant by the word 'history'. History is the discussion of past events based on *written* records; spoken ones do not count, nor do generally agreed verbal records. It can use all sorts of documents, from stone carved hieroglyphs to pieces of toilet paper smuggled out of prison, but it must be written. The content of the document can be an event, a decision or an opinion, none of which is necessarily true.

Playing cards, the type used for playing games in general, are first mentioned late in the fourteenth century, when the Town Council of Regensburg banned their use in 1378. In 1397 their use by the common people during ordinary working days was banned in Paris. Early in the fifteenth century printing from wooden blocks was first practised in Southern Germany. This process was used to print the Bible and playing cards, both of which became available to the masses. In 1415 there is mention of a hand-painted set of Tarot cards prepared for the Duke of Milan. Both ordinary cards and the Tarot cards seem to have spread throughout Europe very rapidly over the next few centuries.

During this period various packs of amusing, decorative and instructive cards appeared in various places all over Europe; interest in the Tarot waxed and waned every forty or fifty years. During the quiet periods it would only be used by Gypsies and fortune-tellers. Then suddenly it would be rediscovered and the demand for packs of these cards would be so great that every little printer would rush out a new pack, rather like hula hoops or skateboards today. That is one of the reasons why there are so many different packs available; each printer would have to prepare his own set of plates, and these would be prepared by a hack draughtsman unversed in the Tarot who would copy out an existing pack *with his own minor changes and additions*. You can imagine what would happen by the time a copy had been made of a copy, and so on. Later on the writers of esoteric, original books, like Lévi, Waite and Crowley, would make their own interpretations of how they felt the cards should look,and so even more different packs appeared. The last ten years have seen a sudden spate of newly inspired decks, and the reprinting of many unsuitable old ones.

None of the early historical references gave any hard and fast indication of where the cards originally came from. Not until the eighteenth century did people start taking the Tarot seriously. This was the Age of Enlightenment, and everything was examined seriously. First came a certain Antoine Court de Gébelin, who wrote a series of books about customs, religion, science and ideas of ancient times, comparing them with their modern equivalents. In volume eight he discussed *The Game of Tarot*, speculating on its ancient Egyptian origins. These books were written in the 1770s, when European scholars were first discovering the huge hoard of Egyptian antiquities. This included enormous numbers of tablets, papyri and walls covered in hieroglyphics, which were obviously writing, but to which nobody could attach any meaning. This was about twenty years before the discovery of the Rosetta stone, which finally allowed the hieroglyphs to be deciphered. During this period all Europe was going mad about 'Egyptiana' and its ideas influenced dress and wallpapers, interior design and furniture, but above all mysticism. Seen in the context of the time, Egypt was as good a choice as any; if de Gébelin had been writing today he would have picked Tibet or the prehistoric Indus Valley.

His ideas were taken up by Alliette, a Parisian who wrote books on the subject in the mid-1780s under the pen-name of Etteilla. He enthusiastically adopted and developed the Egyptian theory, and gained an enormous following. About seventy years later the most famous of French occultists, a certain Alphonse Louis Constant wrote two major books in 1855 and 1856 under the name of Eliphas Lévi. By this time the hieroglyphics had been deciphered, and it was realised that there was nothing in them about the Tarot, so Lévi had to go elsewhere for his mystic source, and he chose to connect the Tarot with the Qabalah. The Qabalah is a Jewish mystical system based on the link between numbers and letters of the Hebrew alphabet. By changing the letters in a name into the corresponding number, it was possible to 'decipher' the mysterious names in the Old Testament to give support to a tremendously complicated vision of the Universe. Again, no hard evidence was offered, only that the system worked. Later on in his career, Lévi became convinced that the cards originated in ancient times in the Middle East, but were actually brought to Europe by the Gypsies.

This brings us to the last major influence in the history of the Tarot, Dr Gerard Encausse who wrote, under the name of Dr Papus, a book called *The Tarot of the Bohemians* in 1889; the Bohemians are what we now call Gypsies. It was well known that the Gypsies had been wandering over the face of the earth for a long time, and could trace their origins to ancient Egypt.

When we examine all the writing on the subject, as far as I have been able to find out, not a single book can quote an authoritative source or even a mention or a hint much before the fourteenth century. There has been a great deal of speculation; it has been related to the ancient Greek mysteries, to the old pre-Christian religions in Europe and around the Mediterranean and linked with witchcraft. Others have discovered Middle Eastern, Qabalistic or Sufi origins, Indian or even Chinese sources. Yet nobody is willing to find or give evidence, and that is why there is so little history of its development or discovery.

Perhaps the history of it doesn't matter, in the same way as the history of the wheel, or fire, is nowhere nearly as important as the fact that we use it every day. Perhaps we feel that if we knew the original intent with which the Tarot had been put together, we could then gain a much better idea of the real meaning of the cards. But are we able to use the wheel, or light a fire, any the worse for knowing nothing about its original inventor?

An even more telling comparison concerns the Quaker religion, which is generally known for its rational, humanistic and idealistic framework. Yet originally the Quakers were known as such because in the revival-type meetings held before and during the rule of the Roundheads they literally 'quaked' and shook as a sign that they were possessed by the Lord, rather as other groups might speak with tongues. Only after the Restoration did they slowly emerge as the group we know today; in earlier days they had to work hard to 'kill' their bad image. Does it really help us to understand present day Quakers if we know their origins? The most important thing is to understand what they are doing now, and what they can and will do in the future.

Similarly, the actual history of the Tarot is not as important as the use you make of it. It may help you, however, if you consider the following story, which is imaginary but can be found in many books on the Tarot.

A long time ago, before the dawn of history, there were ancient civilizations; they are all so long ago that their memory has perished. As you may remember from school, in the Middle East there were a number of these civilizations, each of which rose to a peak, and then crashed because the Barbarians at the Gate conquered it. The common people were enslaved, which merely meant a change of masters, and the upper crust were killed; the priests, who were usually also the civil servants, were often kept alive and in their old jobs, firstly because someone who knew the secret of writing could prove to be useful, and secondly, as the civil service, they were probably the only people who could actually run the country.

You must imagine that the official religion of the outgoing regime had its exoteric and its esoteric sides, something we have already discussed. Initiates would be taught the mystic hidden secrets, and perhaps perform the priestly functions at a later date. The common people were left to their own superstitions, rather in the same way as an Italian peasant will celebrate his Saint's day without knowing exactly why that person became a Saint, or even caring. As long as the Saint provides a good excuse for a Fiesta and looks after the crops and welfare of the parish, that's all he cares about. But the Jesuit priest is expected to go into the history, the mysticism, the ideas and the theory of his religion in order to gain greater understanding. In the same way, in ancient days, the initiate would be taught the inner mysteries, and this esoteric teaching would primarily be designed to help him evolve into a better human being, a saner and healthier person. Each individual would have to learn what being an evolved person was about. Obviously there would have to be a guide to help him, and this was one of the duties of the priests.

Now, when for the umpteenth time the civilization was about to be overrun by a particularly brutal set of barbarians, the priests talked it over, and decided that if they were all to be killed, it would be a shame to lose all that esoteric guidance. They cast about for ways to keep their ideas alive and lasting; stone tablets might be defaced, books might be lost or burnt, and in any case few people could read. Then one of them had the idea of designing a game which people could play but which incorporated all the major elements of the teaching. The uninitiated common people would be playing the game, and thus keep alive the tradition, which would thus stay available for potential candidates for initiation; an esoteric idea under an exoteric guise. The priests were indeed killed, but the cards are still there, and still form a guide, if correctly used and understood, to spiritual development.

We can see that the search to discover the original esoteric meanings of these cards should really serve as a focus in the development of our own evolution. If the above story were really true, then nothing is lost by knowing the veracity or authenticity of this story. If we use the Tarot in modern times to connect our conscious and our subconscious, then it is surely serving the same purpose it was originally intended to serve; we have only changed the terminology.

Chapter 3

ASTROLOGY AND THE TAROT

I have often been asked during the discussions which followed my
lectures why I haven't gone further and studied astrology. Almost as
if they were similar things that every mystic person ought to know.
At first I replied that I didn't see the point of learning too many
things at once; learning the Tarot might take me the first fifty years,
after which I would see. I quoted Confucius, who started his serious
study of the I Ching very late in life, not feeling ready for serious
things until in his seventies.

But I reflected on it, and gradually my viewpoint changed.
Perhaps the study of one might enable me to understand the other;
perhaps I had been too frightened of the complicated arithmetic,
which scared me plain silly. In time I started to regard myself with
some contempt, and settled down with coffee, paper and pencil to
tackle this work. As I progressed I reached a certain amount of
insight as to why astrology seemed so unattractive to me.

Clairvoyance, character analysis, fortune-telling, psychotherapy
and all the other respectable and not so respectable personal sci-
ences can be grouped into two major categories. To the first belong
palmistry, the Tarot, tea-leaf reading and psychoanalysis; to the
second psychology, astrology and numerology. The dividing line is
drawn with regard to their need for the two people involved to be in
physical proximity; the first group needs that interaction, and the
second one doesn't. It is perfectly possible to prepare a chart of
someone who is not in the room, and whom you have never met, but
there is no way to select Tarot cards by post. The astrologers with
whom I have discussed this immediately object that they often have
their subject in the same room when interpreting their chart. This
merely indicates that it is possible, not that it is necessary. After

meeting many people who prefer one or the other of these groups, I gradually realized that their preferred mode reflects their own attitude to touching or being in the emotional field of other people, especially strange people with possibly very different life styles or attitudes.

Many people feel that their ideals ought to dictate their choice of career as counsellor, therapist or fortune-teller with and for other people. To achieve this they train as social workers, psychotherapists, astrologers and the like. But their real personal feelings are that they don't want to touch the body or the psyche of the other person. So they concentrate on those aspects which will allow them to combine both their ideal and their real feelings. Typically an astrologer can be intensely involved with people without ever meeting or seeing them; he can placate his ideals as set out in his consciousness, and yet not be involved with the messy actual contact. Again, we see people who love children, and work with and for them, but never actually cuddle them, or have play-fights; others may be much more adult-oriented, and yet romp all over the living-room with them.

This is not in any way intended to convey contempt or disapproval, it merely reflects a difference between the two types of temperament. It also finally made me realize why I liked the Tarot so much. I just like mucking in.

But it must always be borne in mind that the Tarot reader will be personally involved with the Querent (the person who is being read); they are both part of an interacting spiral. The Reader reacts to the reaction of the Querent to the things the Reader says in response to the Querent's question, and so on. There is in fact 'feedback'.

Now feedback is a term borrowed from cybernetics, which is the study of how things are governed or guided to achieve the ends required in a dynamic system. The simplest way to understand the term feedback is to think about how we steer a bicycle.

Imagine yourself on a bicycle, pedalling merrily along. However carefully we hold the handlebars, sooner or later we swing off course, let us say to the left. Automatically we swing the wheel to the right, and we go on doing so until the bicycle stops going to the left, and begins to go to the right. If it goes too far to the right, we swing the handlebars to the left, till we see that the bicycle is going straight. At no time do we measure our deviation, or decide 'how much' to swing in the opposite direction. We just push the handlebars in the opposite direction from the deviation till we decide it is right.

Here we have a simple cybernetic path. The machine (which consists of the bicycle plus the cyclist) deviates from the chosen direction. The eye sees it and informs the brain which directs the hands to move the steering unit. The eye then checks to see whether the handlebars have moved, and whether the bike is still going to the left, has started to move to the right, or is going straight. The eye then tells the brain what has happened, and the brain issues further instructions to the hands; move more, move less, keep it as is. As the corrections are being made, new deviations crop up, which are dealt with on a continuous basis. In fact, the bike never goes straight; it actually moves in little swings to the left and right which are evened out into one general direction.

If a major deviation occurs (caused perhaps by trying to miss another bicycle coming straight at us), and we correct it with a big swing to the right, and then a smaller correction to the left, till we are riding fairly straight, we speak of a negative feedback. Where, however, the big swing to the left causes us to almost overbalance, we correct with an even bigger swing to the right in a desperate attempt to regain our balance. It is to no avail, the wobbling gets worse and worse, and at last we fall off. This is the situation of positive feedback. Positive feedback is then a situation where the attempt to correct the deviation results in even greater deviations, and so on till disaster occurs.

Having explained feedback, we now see that where there is an intimate relationship between two people, the possibility of feedback reactions operating is strong. The closer two people are, the more likely these feedback effects are; something we have all noticed in situations where two people live in each other's pockets. It can also be seen in the effect of long periods of work on psychiatrists, who have an unusually high incidence of nervous breakdowns and suicides. But even in the single reading of the Tarot spread, very intimate relationships are-possible, and in fact are part of the bond between Reader and Querent. When, then, the feedback becomes positive, the troubles of the Querent can influence the Reader in an unpleasant way. This is the possibility that the astrologer is secretly afraid of and then tries to avoid, whilst yet maintaining his involvement with people.

Yet we will see when discussing the 'Psychic Mirror' that the very accuracy of the Tarot depends on this feedback. Not only do we need to be in touch with ourselves, but also we must be in touch, at a psychic level, with the Querent, and the Querent must be in touch with us.

Chapter 4

THE PSYCHIC MIRROR

Generally speaking the Tarot is approached from a mystical point of view. It is assumed that there is a power in some men which allows them to perceive things which cannot be perceived by less gifted mortals. The ones who have this gift may not have developed it, but by learning how to use the cards they will be able to make use of their exceptional talent. Others, who are less lucky, do not have the gift, and will never develop it, however hard they study and work.

Many people get it firmly drummed in at an early age that they are not artistic. 'Look', they say, 'I can't paint or draw.' True, but then I ask them to look at the way they are dressed or the way they lay a table; these can be done in pleasing ways, or otherwise. They hadn't realized that these were also artistic subjects.

If you, the reader, firmly believe in the greater or lesser talent, then the best method is to buy standard book on the Tarot and a pack of cards, and proceed to find out if you have the talent or not. If you find the correct book with the most authentic meanings you are bound to succeed, provided you have the talent. Obviously, I cannot teach you to grow a talent, or mystical intuition, or gifts. I could describe them, and mention the results, much as I could chronicle the miracles of the Saints.

Now I do not disbelieve in the idea of the mystical approach to the Tarot but, as I explained above, I cannot write about it nor can I tell you how to go about getting hold of some. And wouldn't it be awful to go to all the trouble of learning the Tarot only to find you haven't the talent. The rest of this book will describe how to go about using the Tarot without ever needing to worry whether you have the talent or not.

I will start by explaining that the human mind may be thought of as having three parts. The first one is the Conscious; this is the part that talks, reasons, decides, remembers things, and is generally aware of itself. The second part is the Sub-Conscious; this is the part that feels, and notices all things, and makes the decision as to whether to tell the Conscious or not. The third part is the Un-Conscious; here are the instincts, the reflexes and drives.

The three parts communicate badly with each other, and this is especially so between the conscious and the subconscious. Everything that happens around us gets noticed by our organs of perception, i.e. our eyes, ears, nose, etc. which convert what they notice into electrical signals which are transmitted to the brain. In the brain first of all they are examined by the subconscious to see whether they are important enough to pass on to the conscious. Some signals are important enough, such as the colour of the traffic lights when we are driving a car; others don't matter enough to be passed on, but, and this must be stressed, they do get noticed and stored by the subconscious.

Unimportant signals might be a minute change in the temperature of the air around us, or perhaps a faint noise in the distance. Sometimes a signal comes in which is so laden with non-rational information that our emotions, which are in the subconscious, react first, before our conscious part learns what is going on. We hear someone say something to us and we feel a gush of anger; our hand is ready to hit when suddenly our conscious analyses what is going on, and reminds us that hitting people is wrong, so wrong that we may end up in prison. Some of the information going into the subconscious is so important that it goes directly to the unconscious, and stays there without ever being able to go to the conscious directly. But information reaching the unconscious forms our drives, our needs and urges, which in turn modify our emotions in the subconscious, and which then finally emerge as ideas in our conscious. We try to rationalize our actions, which is nothing other than finding a good reason to do things after we have *already* decided to do them – based on the seemingly irrational impulses welling up from our sub- and unconscious.

In essence, we can say that the subconscious acts as a very good secretary or personal assistant. It knows everything that goes on, but only passes on to the conscious such information as it thinks will be what the conscious would want. This would be a good arrangement except that the emotions, which are very much part of the subconscious, colour heavily the opinions of the personal assistant as to what the boss wants to know. The boss is often unaware of this bias, and so doesn't realize what is being withheld.

Very small children, and the more intelligent animals, have a very good connection between their conscious and their subconscious. It is very difficult to tell a small child a lie about your feelings towards that small child; it is also difficult to fool an animal. You may be in the same room as your dog, who badly wants to go for a walk. Several times you get up to go to the kitchen, and each time your dog looks up and whines softly; it is his signal for indicating his needs. But the dog doesn't actually get up. Then suddenly you yourself feel like a small walk; you get up, and this time the dog is at the door of the room before you are. Somehow, the dog knows.

Konrad Lorenz, the animal psychologist, tells of an acquaintance of his who had a remarkably intelligent parrot. It could not only say words, like many other parrots, but could even understand some, like 'Good-bye', and use them correctly. Many visitors came to see this remarkable animal, and on being told that it would say 'Good-bye' when they left, immediately wanted to test this. They put on coats, hats and gloves, shook hands and left through the door. Nothing happened. But hours later, when, after an interesting chat, the visitor really got up to leave, the parrot would interrupt to say 'Good-bye'! The parrot knew, even when the visitor had forgotten its existence.

Children often 'feel' adults in the same way. When told to shake hands with the nice 'Uncle' Charlie, they refuse. Their mother will shake her head, being unable to understand what has got into the child, he's usually so nice and friendly. Some mothers will punish their children for such anti-social behaviour, others will just indicate their disapproval. Gradually, as the child grows up, it begins to be borne in upon the conscious that to react by indicating its feelings directly is 'not nice' and leads to disapproval; the subconscious makes a note of it and from now on simply doesn't tell the conscious nasty suspicions about Uncle Charlie. The censor is set up, and will get stronger and more ubiquitous day by day, and more difficult to pierce as time goes by.

The subconscious continues to notice things. It notices the smile on the face not matching the coldness of the eyes. It notices the very slight hesitation when the nice 'Uncle' Charlie talks to your young, pretty and recently widowed mother in ever such a nice way. The conscious has learned to ignore such things, or rather the subconscious has learned that such things are not to be brought to the conscious' notice. But that doesn't stop the subconscious having feelings about matters. And it is these feelings and ideas in the subconscious that the Tarot tries to bring to the attention of the conscious. Let us make a model of the Tarot:

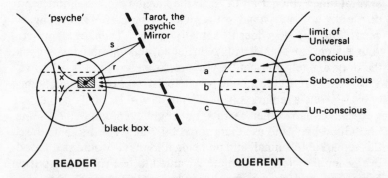

The two large circles are the minds or psyche of the two individuals facing each other across the table over a Tarot spread. The Querent talks to the Reader, asking him to reflect and interpret certain problems that the Querent needs a solution to. It is the conscious of the Querent that does the talking and formulates and utters the words. The subconscious of the Reader picks up the words, sorts them out, and sends up to the conscious those things which it has learned through many years of practice will not be rejected, spurned or disapproved. The rest of the message stays with the subconscious, and some of it may be sent to the unconscious, to be processed; after processing some of it may come back to the subconscious which may, after reprocessing send some of it up to the conscious. In any event, only part of the material sent out by the Querent reaches the Reader's conscious.

The information sent out by the Querent's conscious is marked by arrow 'a'. In addition, there is other material sent out by the Querent's subconscious, marked by the arrow 'b'. We do, and say, things in such a way as to be totally unaware of what we are doing. These unaware expressions of ourselves can be read, or at least some of them can be read, by people who have trained themselves to be aware; they call it 'body language'. The next time you are in a situation where people of opposite sexes mingle informally, as in a pub or a party, watch the way that typically the young man will move about restlessly while 'chatting up a bird' till he has manoeuvred the girl with her back up against a wall. When he has got her into this position where she cannot evade him any further, he then stands nonchalantly with his arm resting against the wall, to one side of her but not touching; in his other hand he holds a cigarette or a drink. She cannot, and probably does not want to, back away or move sideways; his arm clearly signals that he would like to wrap it round her, but doesn't feel encouraged enough yet to do so. His subconscious signals his real ideas using body language; her subconscious is easily receiving them.

The subconscious of the Querent therefore also sends out signals which are picked up by the subconscious of the Reader. Moreover, the unconscious isn't going to be left out of the act, and also adds factors which go into the Reader's subconscious; these are shown by the arrow marked 'c'. Typical unconscious signals are 'fear-smells', speeding up of heartbeat and sweating under stress; nowadays we have lie detectors to measure these signals, but in fact your subconscious can also notice these things and draw the appropriate conclusions.

We see that the Reader's subconscious is in fact inundated with streams of data; as it comes in it is processed through a little 'black box'. We don't quite know *how* the black box works, but we do know *what* it does. It sorts out all the data coming in, and routes it either to other sections or keeps it. Only a small proportion actually goes to the conscious, marked by arrow 'x'. A larger proportion goes to the unconscious, marked by arrow 'y' and the rest stays in the subconscious, where it helps to regulate the exact working of the 'black box'. If we could only see all that goes into that black box, what a story we could tell.

This is where the Tarot comes in. We cannot connect directly with our subconscious, but if somewhere there were a mirror which would allow us to 'see around the corner' into our mystic part, then we would be able to know far more. The Tarot may be thought of as a half-silvered mirror which allows us to 'look through a glass darkly' at our subconscious. The glass is half-silvered, which means that the coating on the back, which is normally thick enough to give a perfect reflection, is in this case only a thin layer; thick enough to give some reflection, and thin enough so as to allow us to look through it at the signals coming from the Querent.

The mirror image of our subconscious is therefore not very clear, just as the images received through the Tarot are not very clear. The images are smoky, reversed or upside down, but still they are much better than nothing. Arrows 's' and 'r' show the information reaching us through the Tarot. We can see things, but they are on the threshold of perception. If we want to see something a little more clearly, we must focus on a particular area. That is why we often ask a specific question. The deeper the question, the better the focus, and the more clearly we can see. Focussing the question is a very important part of the Tarot technique, and I will return to it later on in the book.

You must not imagine that the exchange of information stops here. As the Reader talks about what he sees, the words from the Reader's conscious will be received by the Querent's subconscious, as well as signals from the Reader's subconscious and unconscious. These signals will be processed by the Querent's subconscious, and the relevant parts will be sent on to the conscious and unconscious of the Querent. Each part of the Querent will react; the conscious will perhaps interrupt or even disagree, the subconscious will change posture or cough, and the unconscious will blush or sweat. These changes in the Querent are normally considered as reactions, but really they are signals at a subconscious level, to the Reader. These signals are received by the Reader's subconscious and form further input data so as to further the accuracy of the Reader. I must emphasize that this is not a conscious confidence trick, but that the Reader is totally unaware of what is going on.

Lastly you will notice the two large semi-circles marked 'limit of Universal'. The Universal is what might be called 'God' or 'Mother Nature' or whatever; the area that is common to both the semi-circle and the circle drawn to represent our psyche is what might be called the soul. Only a little part crosses the conscious part of our psyche, which is why we are not really aware of having a soul. Our subconscious is much more aware of the soul. The purpose of any form of self-evolution is to lower the line, or loosen the line, between our conscious and our subconscious, in order that we become more fully aware of our soul. The Tarot is one such measure; and after using it for a long time, we notice that as we get more proficient in its use, we need it less in order to see things. Our dependence on the mirror becomes smaller as we grow, till in the end we don't need it any more.

part two

Chapter 5

CONFUSION

It was my custom at the beginning of each new class in learning to read the Tarot to ask each person, as they came in to join the group, to tell us about how they first came across the cards.

Many people, myself included, were first introduced to the Tarot by someone who had a pack and tried them out at a party, or perhaps after a dinner party; we became intrigued, tried it out ourselves and ended up by buying a pack.

Other people were given a pack by a friend or a relative for Christmas or their birthday – something nice to have round the house. A third group of people wander into a shop, perhaps a little bored or perhaps with money to burn in their pockets; they notice a pack on a shelf, and suddenly remember vaguely that this is something they've heard about. So they buy a pack and take it home to try it out.

We open the pack, and out come the shiny plastic-finished new cards, with their quaint drawings and curious names. Some packs come with a big, beautifully illustrated coffee-table book, but most come with a little slip of paper which attempts to tell you in 500 words or so exactly what it is all about. They will give a meaning to all the cards, perhaps one or two spreads, and now it is up to us.

After each card, the little slip of paper will list a number of meanings, such as:

> EMPRESS: Action, plan, undertaking, abundance, growth, beauty, success, creation, motherhood, a benefactress.
> PRIESTESS: Intuition, supportive female force, wisdom, understanding, passion, the woman of one's life, helpfulness.

If you are faced with such a choice of ideas about each card, and moreover, if some of the meanings given to one card don't look all that different from the meanings mentioned under another card, then there's bound to be some confusion.

At this point, a lot of people give up; they would pefer to wait till they come across a book, or a person, who *does* know. But other people try using the cards, and picking one of the meanings given to the card they are talking about. It seems to work quite well, and so they carry on. But all the time they feel a little unsure, and they are looking for some way of finding a more authoritative version; after all, no one can expect a miracle from a little slip of paper written by some hack working for a pittance doled out by a commercial printer of playing cards.

One day or another, the novice comes across a book on the subject. These days, most public libraries have at least one book on the subject, and many have several. Suburban book shops offer several to the interested public – some are beautifully illustrated books with many pictures and photographs, but expensive. Others are cheap paperbacks, with cruder line drawings, but with more words. If you really start looking, then you will find anything up to thirty or forty books currently in print.

All of them will give you a history of the cards – we have seen in the first section of this book how accurate and how relevant that is. They then start to give the meanings of the cards, usually going into great detail about the Major Arcana, less so for the Minor. Finally, they finish up with some typical spreads. When these books talk about the meanings of the cards, they will liberally sprinkle the text with words like 'usually', 'generally', 'traditionally' and 'customarily'. The more heavy-weight types will devote a chapter or so to each card of the Major Arcana, with lots of ideas drawn from Roman, Greek, Babylonian and other mythologies; they will talk about witchcraft, matriarchy or alchemy. At the end of five or so pages about, say, the Empress, the reader is now thoroughly confused. The light-weight books generally solve that particular problem by providing a little résumé of the principal ideas associated with each card; now we are back to our little list given with the pack of cards.

But there is one significant difference – the meanings given don't look anything like the first list. What is worse, each book will differ from every other one. Some of the ideas match, but too many differ.

The novice gets more and more uncertain, and eventually puts down the book with the idea of taking it up later on in life. Life's too short to spend it on following up some complicated and ambiguous book.

There are specialist books on the subject which try to collect all the various ideas on the meanings. They either describe, or show pictures of, all the different packs in existence; they also set down all the different meanings given by different authorities. As a piece of historical research, this shows that a lot of effort has been made. But it does not leave the reader any the wiser. If the purpose of making this collection (or of any collection) is to show how persistent the scholar or collector has been, how patient he has been over the years, then we can admire that patience, that persistence. But that still doesn't help us to understand the purpose of the cards.

Confusion still reigns. The number of books grows steadily year by year, and each book adds to the confusion. Some are considered more accurate or better researched; these will become standard reference works, and perhaps the hope is that if enough people spend enough time then eventually the result will be that the original esoteric knowledge is very closely approximated. It is just a matter of working on it.

I think the amount of work and the number of words devoted to the subject is magnificent; but I don't think it is relevant. It is rather as if we started to study literature by spending more and more time putting together dictionaries and writing textbooks on grammar. Yet if we look at any of the big names in literature, we notice that in fact they are the ones who decided the spelling and the grammar (of which more later). While there are schools of creative writing, real down-to-earth full-time writers will usually tell you that they learned to write by *doing*, by practising ways of setting down words and sending them in to editors till one day some kind person bought the piece. At times the ideas of the writers are so interesting, that the grammar and the spelling don't matter too much.

To quote the standard expression:

'Larst week I coodn't spell orther, now I are one'

As more and more teachers are beginning to realize, and to put into practice, writing (and for that matter painting or any other art form) is about the expression of ideas that are fresh and real, and *not* the setting out correctly of approved standard forms.

When applied to the Tarot, this means that in my opinion the cards are to be used to convey some of the feelings and ideas, arising out of our unconscious and subconscious, to another person. In order to do this, we will have to understand that using the cards is a way of doing things rather like riding a bicycle – something that can be learned but not taught.

To take the analogy further, what I suspect has happened is that as each person learned to ride his bicycle, he described the way that he himself learned as the standard method applicable to everyone. Yet it is the bicycle riding that is important, not the way to learn to ride a bicycle.

It was precisely the bewildering number of 'standard' definitions and the conflicts, ambiguities and vague ideas which set me on the whole trail of learning to understand the Tarot. In a sense the material in the section of the book that follows is a recapitulation of my own progress in learning. So here follows some background material which I hope you will have the tenacity to follow; if it proves difficult, remember I couldn't even find another person to follow.

Chapter 6

VOCABULARY

Here I am writing a book about the Tarot. I sit behind my typewriter, and set down my thoughts in the hope that the ideas I have can be arranged in such a way that you, the reader, will understand them. In order to do so, I am using 'words', which are really sounds, or in this case marks on paper, which have some meaning attached to them. A very complicated idea really; just to show you how complicated it really is, try to think about this idea *without using words*.

Even more interesting, human beings vary greatly in their level of intelligence, and yet all of them use words to think. A few animals have 'words' which they use to inform other members of their species about events or conditions (bees are an obvious example), but most animals can only convey feelings. Feelings can consist of fear, surprise, pleasure, hunger, anger, all of which are expressed through various different noises which animals make. Many animals have a vocabulary of perhaps ten or twenty different feelings; animal psychologists such as Konrad Lorenz have spent their lives learning to recognize them.

Human beings have vocabularies that vary from 1,500 words to 20,000 words. A very simple Stone Age tribe will have fewer words than a professor of literature. Obviously, someone living and working in a university needs many more words to express the increasingly complicated ideas that are generated. But *having* a big vocabulary is not the same as using a large vocabulary. People differ in the number of words they 'know'; that is, words they can spell, words they've seen and can recognize even though they're not quite sure what they mean. But 'knowing' a word is not exactly the same as being able to use the word. Most of us use far fewer words than we know. For instance, a given person may know something like 20,000 words, but will use only about 5,000 of these in most of his discussions. Another man who knows 4,000 words will perhaps use only 1,500 in daily speech. Perhaps if he works in a place where a display of intelligence is frowned upon, such as a factory or work-shop, he will actually use perhaps only 200 words; he will use these a lot, and the others only in the course of a month or so.

In fact, there is a group of words, numbering about 850, which includes four active verbs, about fourteen auxiliary verbs, about 150 adjectives and adverbs, and the rest composed of nouns, which can be used to express all ideas in the English language. It has been used to translate the Bible, and to write stories. It is called Basic English and uses only perfectly normal English words. It looks perfectly normal, it is very easy to read, and doesn't look artificial or strange. We could, from now on, just use this group of 850 words and no other. It would make life so much easier, since then we wouldn't have to know all those long, unusual or complicated words.

But we still would have to know those 850 words. We would still have to agree with each other as to their exact meaning. Oh, but that's easy, I can almost hear someone say – we just use a diction-ary. Most of us have used a dictionary at some time or another. We use them often to check the spelling of a word. At other times, we check on the exact meaning, perhaps to settle a bet with a friend. You look it up in the Webster's; the friend looks it up in Funk and Wagnall's; both of you come up with a triumphant cry of 'See, I was right!' You settle the matter by looking it up in the official Oxford English dictionary, a pleasant little piece of writing about 20 volumes long. But how does the official dictionary know?

We use our little or big vocabularies all day long, and don't have any troubles. Sometimes we don't quite know how to express our-selves; if we are lucky, we hear or read something which applies exactly to what were trying to say. Sometimes, someone uses a word we don't know; then we have to look it up if we want to know the exact meaning.

Perhaps the unknown word is 'synergy'. I think I know what the word means, and in fact I have used the word in my writing and my speech any number of times. But there was a first time, when I had to look it up – in a dictionary. Perhaps you know the word already (can you remember the first time you came across the word?) or perhaps you need to look it up. Do so, right now; I'll wait till you have found a meaning.

In fact, while I was waiting, I looked it up myself:

Synergy – n. A state of affairs in which the effect of the sum of the parts is greater than the sum of the effects of the individual parts.

Now that we have 'defined' the word in terms of other words, we feel happier. We might even understand the meaning. But suppose that we were very young and not very well-read; we might not know some of the words like 'affairs' or 'state'. A grown-up might explain that 'state of affairs' means 'things as they are'; we could go on like this and explain all the complicated words using simpler words. The simpler words would be understood by eight-year-olds, but might still be too complicated for four-year-olds. So we find even simpler words. But when we have explained everything in words and ideas suitable for a bright two-year old, we come to a barrier. How do you explain words and their meaning to a very young child? How do you tell a baby to say 'Mama' when he sees her, or 'Food' when he is hungry?

Very young babies make random noises and movements shortly after being born. A few movements and noises are instinctive and automatic; that is, all normal children make them, and in the same way, and in order to obtain the same response. For instance, all children cry when they are dissatisfied, when they want something or don't want something. But gradually, babies realize that some movements or noises work better than other ones; if they smile, Mummy picks them up and cuddles them. So, even that tiny baby uses its little organic computer to calculate that smiling gets certain results. From then on it is a small step, but a very important one, to smile when it wants to be picked up. Baby smiles; baby gets picked up. Aha! From being a random movement done occasionally for no particular reason the smile becomes a calculated action – it becomes a 'word' in its vocabulary.

Later, the baby starts making noises. Gurgling, and Mama gurgles back. Don't laugh, this is one of the most important things any human can do. The baby smiles and gurgles, and Mama picks baby up! She makes a noise, over and over again. One day, baby makes a similar noise, or at least Mama thinks it is similar. Immediately, Mama is very pleased, so pleased that baby gets even more attention than ever. Baby's organic computer calculates that if it really wants to be picked up, it should smile and say 'Mama'. Baby has learned its first word.

And already the first semantic misunderstanding has arisen. The mother thinks that the baby means 'Hallo Mother, I love you', when the child says 'Mama'. What in fact baby probably means is 'Please pick me up and cuddle me/change my nappy/feed me'. This confusion doesn't matter much at this stage, because when the mother hears 'Mama' she does cuddle/change/feed the baby.

The baby starts learning some more words, like 'Dada', 'No', 'More' and 'Don't-like-it'. Each of these words is learned through copying the sounds made by Mama, and then seeing what effects these sounds have in different contexts.

The next stage is for the child to start using simple operatives, things such as verbs; typical verbs of interest to a very small child such as 'want' or 'like'. Again, these are learned through the mother asking things like 'Does Baby *want* some chocolate'. If baby says 'No', baby gets none; if 'Yes' then baby gets some. Through its context, baby learns verbs, and negatives like 'baby *doesn't* want'. The child builds up a vocabulary of twenty words or so, and strings them together, as in 'Don't-like-it' + 'Food' + 'More' to achieve a simple sentence like 'I don't want any more food' Mother and child may disagree on this, but they both understand the meaning of the phrase.

This is followed by the 'What's that?' phase. It gradually builds up a larger and larger vocabulary, and eventually it will talk fluently, and express itself in the way proper to his or her class and station in the context of its native culture.

Having followed, very sketchily, the first beginnings in the formation of your vocabulary, we can now proceed to discuss how you learn new words as a grown-up.

First of all, we must realize that it is no good being told that a word means 'such-and-such'. That is on a level with being told that this piece of music is 'beautiful', because it was written by Tchaikovsky and is 'classical'. One person might think it was far too high-brow, whilst another would mutter 'romantic nonsense' and switch to something interesting like Beethoven's later violin sonatas, or early Schoenberg.

Next we must try out the word in different contexts. It would be grammatically correct to say 'the lightning flash crawled across the sky', but it would not sound quite right. Next time we might try using the word 'crawled' in a phrase like 'time crawled slowly through the hot summer afternoon', and this time everyone nods their head, and drops off to sleep. We will gradually experiment to find out the exact differences of nuance from other words which also mean something like 'to move slowly'; words like 'to creep' or 'to slither'.

It would help, perhaps, if we knew how a dictionary is written. Most of us have a dictionary somewhere about the house; perhaps a paperback or cheap edition with fifty- or sixty-thousand words; if the dictionary is honest, it will mention that the definitions come from the 'Oxford English Dictionary' a pleasant bit of writing which takes up a seven-foot shelf, and in which you can find all the words ever used in the English Language; at least, all the words in use before that particular volume was printed. By the time all the volumes are written and printed, some of the words are out of date, or their meanings have changed. New words will have come into use. So there is a continual programme of revision. But how did they originally decide on the meanings of any word? You know, sometimes when you talk with people, you get the idea that they have decided that some time ago, maybe round Genesis Ch.1, verse 3, somebody formed a committee which drew up a list of words to be used by the English speaking peoples (and all other *sensible* people) which would cover all matters up to the invention of the TV, when a new word had to be invented. But that was all right, since it used Latin and Greek, which, although not really as good as English, were at least classical.

Well, in fact, the first dictionaries were written by one man, or perhaps a small group of men, who just sat down and wrote down all the words they knew, together with the meaning they decided on. This was necessary, since firstly one has to start somewhere, and secondly, the *idea* of a dictionary had to be tried out. But it wasn't very scientific, and it was very personal. For instance, we all know people who are quite certain that a particular word of which they are very fond, has a meaning of which they are quite sure; nobody else agrees, and when you refer to a dictionary which agrees with you, and not with the obstinate fool, why, he turns round and says that the dictionary has got it wrong. You can imagine what would happen if such a man were to write a dictionary! It is much better left to people who *really* know what words mean. But perhaps such a man also has opiniated ideas – and in fact, perhaps everyone of us has an opinionated idea or two. There must be another method, and in fact there is.

Imagine a musty old Victorian house somewhere in England. Inside sits the Chief Editor. He has been appointed to compile the definitive dictionary of all time. He has made a collection of all the words anybody has ever seen; there are all the dictionaries of the English language ever published, together with French, Dutch, German, Latin, Greek dictionaries, since many common English words are 'borrowed' from these foreign languages. He has perhaps ten or so assistants, scattered round the house.

The first thing to be done is to make a list of all the words to be found in the existing dictionaries. He doesn't copy out the meanings, just the words, in alphabetical order. And, if over the next fifty or a hundred years, while they're working on the dictionary, they come across any new ones, they add them to the list. We'll come to the method of finding new words in a minute – just now we only have his long list.

Our editor has perhaps ten or so full-time assistants, but he has hundreds of other people working for him; these other assistants are people who spend much of their time reading books. Perhaps they are invalids with time on their hands, or librarians or scholars. Each of these assistants is assigned a word, and whenever he comes across that word, in *any* book he reads, he makes a note of the title, author, date and the context in which the word was used. Every now and then, he mails the editor all the little slips of paper he has collected on that word; the editor puts them into a shoe-box. There may be several people checking out that same word, and they will be doing so over twenty or thirty years. Incidentally, they will also be sending him any unusual words they come across, words not seen in any dictionary they possess, on the off-chance it is a word not to be found anywhere in any dictionary, but which *is* used by a few people.

Eventually, after many years, the shoe-box is full, and they have finished with the previous word. The editor gets out all the slips of paper, reads them all and removes duplicates. He then forms little groups of slips where the context shows that the different writers who used that word all have roughly the same idea. Some words have only one meaning – such a word is 'Doge', meaning the chief magistrate of Republican Venice. Other words, like 'Dog', the word immediately next to it in my home dictionary, have 16 main meanings, and combine with 50 or so other words. Most of these things you can point to or draw; abstract qualities or ideas are even harder – words such as 'love' or 'ordinary'. The editor has to make decisions such as to how many piles there are to be, and where each quotation fits in. He has still a chance to be opinionated, but much less so. Eventually he will sort out all contributions, and then pick out one, usually the oldest example, to serve as a typical example of that particular use of that particular word. Each typical use of a given word is set down, and forms the entry next to the word. Now you can understand why the dictionary is so big. It has to contain, not just *a* meaning, no, it has to contain an example of *all* the meanings, together with date, author, book and context.

Now this enormous dictionary is not very useful if you want to look up a word. First of all it is so big that you couldn't keep it easily to hand. It is also obviously enormously expensive. Thirdly, it doesn't give you an answer to the question of what a word means; it only tells you how other people have used the word, and leaves the choice to you.

It is the smaller 'household' dictionaries which use the big dictionary to make up their own list of words. They will produce the dictionary that will be useful to most people – small, cheap and above all, one with direct *statements* as to the meanings. The household dictionary doesn't give the whole truth, but it gives as much of the truth as is necessary in everyday life.

We must bear in mind that when we write or speak, or even think, we generate ideas using the words we know. It is not as if we think of an idea, and then open a dictionary to find words with which to express it (actually, we do do this when we wish to say something in a foreign language). We can only think using the words which we know, or half-know, already. So how do we put together this vocabulary?

Just like the editor of the dictionary. We read and listen to other people – we do it all our lives, starting as a baby. Some words we begin to use, because we find them useful. That is because the object or the feeling occurs often in our lives. Other words we forget or don't notice, because we hardly ever use them. After all, how often do you need the word 'entasis', unless you are an architectural historian or a Scrabble fanatic?

If you want to find out what a word means, and how to use it, you must first of all try to remember when you first heard the word, the person using it and in what context. Then try to remember all the other times you have heard it, and what meaning that word seemed to have on those occasions. This can be very difficult if you are trying to dredge up memories of twenty years ago.

It might be easier to try it in a foreign language. Most of us have learned some French at school; we had to learn long lists of words, and correct grammar, and read inane stories about the Family Lebrun. But it didn't really help us when driving the family car through the streets of Paris trying to find the *pension*.

You might try buying a French newspaper, perhaps several. Start reading it, and pretty soon you'll come across a word you don't know. Don't look it up, just continue reading the other words you *do* know. You will probably come across the word again; by the time you've met it three or four times in different article, I think you will understand it. Look Ma, no dictionary!

By now, it should be clear that if we want to get to know a word we have to find a number of instances where it is used, to get a number of people's opinions of the meaning of the word; we have to use the word ourselves and see what effect it has on people. Just looking it up in a dictionary doesn't really help us find the 'true' meaning of a word.

In the same way, reading a long list of the meanings of a card in the Tarot doesn't give us a true meaning of that card. We will go on in the next chapter about true meanings, and how to find them, but first I want you to try out the Dictionary Game.

THE DICTIONARY GAME

The best way of playing this game is with a group of people, between seven and ten or so. A number of words is chosen equal to the number of people in the group, eight words if there are eight people, and so on. Choose one or more of the following words, or similar ones if you like:

bread	salt	hand
sword	rose	mouth
fish	fire	shoe
cross	paper	lamp
time	book	path

When you have chosen the eight words you will use (or whatever number is applicable) ask each person in the room to write down in one sentence what they think the definition of each word should look like. It may be a practical, a poetical or mystical definition; it can be one everybody agrees on, or a very personal one. Never mind, just set it down.

When everyone is finished, each person in the room becomes an editor, the editor of one of those words. All the definitions of, say, 'fish', are given to one person. Incidentally, this is an area where the leader of such a group can be subtle. Try giving all the definitions of 'time' to a person who is never on time, the definitions of 'mouth' to a person who talks too much.

Each editor sorts out all the definitions into two, or at the most, three groups; each group should consist of definitions with roughly similar meanings, or with a similar way of looking at the word. The editor now writes down a single sentence for each group which should say all the things that the individual slips of paper have said. This stage should finish with two or three long sentences.

Next the editor looks at the three long sentences, and tries to make one long sentence combining the three. This can be very difficult, and each editor may have to choose to leave something out – but don't leave out too much. Take your time over this stage, but try to combine as much as possible.

Having achieved the one sentence, the editor tries to reduce it to a catch-phrase, i.e. one or two words which make a short phrase that is easy to remember.

Lastly, the editor tries to reduce all the information to one single word.

At the close of the game, each editor reports his work, and goes through all the stages; other people discuss his choices. There is no reason why this game shouldn't be played several times in an evening.

If you are a single person, you will have to take a list of words, and just ask friends and people you meet to give you definitions to work on. The game will lack the discussion of your choices, so that even two people 'interviewing' other people will have an advantage if they can discuss it with each other.

Example:

The word chosen was 'Riddle'.

Here are some of the answers given by different people:

* Mystery, but one that can be solved by application
* A group of words or a sentence used to activate a person's mind or brain
* A question that focuses the mind
* Something one asks people – sometimes as a puzzle or a game
* Mysterious question
* An obscure sentence with a hidden meaning
* They make you think, and like life, the answers are often in front of your nose but you can't see them
* Something I believe to be unanswerable until you find the answer.

From these eight ideas, three main strands emerged:

1 it is a mysterious puzzling question
2 it focuses the mind through required activity
3 the answer is at the same time hidden and obvious

This can be summed up in one long sentence:

'A riddle is a puzzle which focuses the mind through the activity required to find the answer which is at the same time hidden and obvious.'

Trying to reduce this long unwieldy sentence to a shorter phrase, I came up with—

'Mind – change activator'

—and I realised this was very clumsy;

suddenly, I saw the real mystical meaning and wrote it down:
CATALYST.
And that is what it is to me – a device to change the way you think about something, but which doesn't get used up in the process. It can go on changing other people's minds without ever being used up. And in trying to answer the riddle our minds can be set up to change their behaviour. When Gautama was faced with the riddle of why people died, or were ill or poor, he started his path to becoming the Buddha.

This game has an old history to it. It is said that one day a wise man was accused of heresy, the penalty for which was death. He was arrested and taken before a panel of religious judges. When he was asked to defend himself, he called for pen, paper and ink, and asked each of the judges to write down their definition of the word 'bread'. As you can imagine, they all wrote down something different. The wise man read them all out, and said sternly:

> 'When you can all agree on what exactly bread is, then perhaps you can all agree on what heresy is. Until then, I suggest you will be so humble as to allow everyone their own opinion about God.'

The story ends with the release of the wise man; somehow I don't think it is a very true story. But the point *does* hold true; only when we know that the meaning of a word is a matter of opinion are we able to see the other person's point of view. Reading the Tarot is a matter of seeing points of view – your own and those of the Querent.

Chapter 7

SYMBOLS

I want you to think of a symbol. It can be any symbol you like, but try to think of an important, powerful, universal symbol. Perhaps you will think of a cross. It is a very important symbol, and has meaning for everyone. But has it the same meaning for everyone? If we look at the last two thousand odd years, we will note the arguments and the shouting, the wars and the persecutions which have arisen out of that symbol. Not because people were for or against the cross, but because people differed on what the symbol meant. Albigensians, Quakers, Huguenots, Methodists, Papists were all labels hung on to people who had an unorthodox idea as to the meaning of the cross. And the labels were hung by people who had other ideas on this same cross. Yet we speak glibly of the cross as a Universal Symbol!

Having chosen a symbol, we must now look at some of the ideas associated with that symbol. The cross could be:
* a symbol of Christ's compassion for Man
* a symbol of the oppression by the clergy or even the inquisition
* a symbol of pain, the pain of crucifixion
* a symbol of courage, of those who die for their convictions
* the symbol for so many things, almost as many as there are people in this world.

In fact, if we look at any well-known internationally recognized 'symbol', and study its meaning as set out by authors, priests, experts and just dumb ordinary people who die for their little symbol, we will come to the conclusion that any given symbol has an infinite variety of ideas associated with it. The symbol is universal, but the exact meaning of the symbol is individual.

I must now digress a little to talk about an aspect of psychology which studies the way we perceive things and recognize them for what they are.

Sometimes you will see, in a colour supplement or a puzzle book, or even the back of some soap powder packet, a little game in which you are shown some photographs of very common objects taken from an unusual angle. You are asked to guess what they are. It may take you a little while, and then suddenly, you see it. Oh yes, you say, that is a clothes-peg, or a pair of scissors. The interesting thing is that before you 'see' it, you cannot 'see' it even partially; after you've seen and recognized it, it isn't puzzling anymore. We recognize something either 'not at all', or 'completely' ; very rarely do we only partially recognize something.

But when we start looking closely at how we *do* recognize objects, we discover that we have, hidden in our brains, a sort of pattern book, in which are shown all the major varieties of objects. Such a pattern-book can't have too many pages, or else we would have too many things to remember; so we only have patterns of the most important things in our lives. These 'important things' provide the major categories, and we then remember the minor categories *by the ways in which they differ* from the major ones.

For instance, let us take the idea of 'car'. We recognize a 'car' by the following facts:
* it has four wheels
* it is very shiny, with bright shiny paint and chrome
* the top half is mostly glass, the bottom mostly metal
* it is about shoulder high, and perhaps two-to-three times as long as a man

Now that doesn't mean that every time we see a strange object we start checking it against our check-list to see if it is a car. No, in fact the reverse happens; we recognize the object as a car *unless* one of the items listed isn't so.

If, for instance, most of the top as well as the bottom is metal, then it isn't a car, but a van. If it has six wheels and is much bigger, then it is a bus. If it has only two wheels, it is probably a caravan. The pattern-book lists 'car' but not 'caravan', 'lorry', 'van' etc.; these are obtained by checking the differences against the master pattern.

Now notice that in this very brief description of how we recognize the object 'car', I haven't talked at all about what a car does, what it is used for, how you make one, and all the other practical items. I haven't given a *meaning* of the word 'car' (if you like, a definition), yet there is a description of how the brain is thought to recognize a 'car'.

At one time in my life I lived in a street with lots of houses which looked very similar, almost as similar as one car to another if they were the same make and colour. Just as cars, after a few years, begin to show bumps and dents in different places, have different stickers, so these houses had different trees, slightly different finishes; some had been repainted recently, while others were looking shabby. But all in all, most people needed to look at the number on the front gate to know which was their house.

Imagine my astonishment to watch my three-year-old daughter walking up the road with me, and suddenly running ahead to beat me to the front door. She couldn't read the number, and when questioned later she could not tell me how she knew which was *her* house. Yet she made no mistake, then or ever. She recognized the house by 'fixing' its image in her pattern-book; the other houses looked very much like it, but in each case there was something slightly wrong about it. She rejected the wrong ones till she found a match for her pattern-book; she was home. She had identified her symbol.

This is where we go back to our symbols. We recognize our symbols as being important, as being master patterns. Their meanings cannot be recognized, because meanings are just lists of words strung together like beads on a wire. The most obvious example of these necklaces of words are the catechisms which we are forced to learn by rote long before we know the meanings of the words. And not just the catechism of a church; in fact I'm thinking of things like 'a circle is the locus of a point at a fixed distance from another point moving on a single plane'. Yet we all have an idea of what a circle *is*, and would instantly recognize one if we came across one.

Up to now we have talked of symbols like the cross and the circle – concrete physical items whose appearances can be described mathematically. Their *meanings* are much more diffuse and much less easily pinned down. Whole books and libraries have been devoted to setting out what people feel that these symbols mean; as we mentioned earlier, wars have been fought and are still being fought. Why is it that a symbol is so potent?

You might like to think of a symbol as a physical, concrete expression of something inside you that is vague, ill-defined and nebulous. You can't say exactly what you feel, perhaps you cannot find the words for it, or perhaps there *are* no words. But if you can point to a thing and say that it is like that thing, you are on the way to creating a symbol.

Symbols usually start their life by being used to define a feeling. A small child feels the need to cuddle something, and picks up a doll. The cuddling of the doll gives the child an opportunity to be protective to something smaller and, in so doing, affirms the child's ability to protect something even more helpless than itself. The child feels stronger, and more secure now that it has expressed its feeling of being *able* to protect. At first, the act of picking up the doll is an expression of an internal need. Later, the sight of a doll will give her this security. And later still, mention of the word 'doll' will symbolize this feeling of security. The doll has become a symbol.

Now the doll is an individual symbol. It applies only to the person who owned the original doll and grew up thinking of that doll as meaning security. Another person might attach a totally different meaning to the word doll. It might be a person who was never allowed to have dolls as a child, and who now sees dolls as symbolizing unattainable ideals. You yourself can think of many others.

Symbols like the cross or the circle are symbols that were important to our forebears. They were so important that they were handed down from generation to generation. The symbol stayed the same, but its meaning changed. The symbol is universal, but its meaning is individual.

* * *

If we look at the individual cards of the Major Arcana, we will see a succession of images. There will be old men, young men, a devil, beautiful women, a tower, and so on. Each of these is a symbol that stands for a range of ideas. It is as if the little doll we were talking about was drawn on a card, so that every time the owner of that doll saw the card, she would think of the security and ability to protect that it meant. That is, if the person seeing the doll were to be the same person who used to hug her doll. If the person who was never allowed to have a doll were to see a card with a drawing of a doll on it, that person would think of the yearning desire for something beyond reach. We can see that each person attaches a different meaning to the card.

Just now, I was talking about the symbol on the Tarot card as being something that is intimately connected to the individual. There are many people for whom the image of a doll has no very potent meaning – they can take it or leave it. To them the sight of a racing car might be a very potent symbol, something which would leave the doll-fancier totally cold.

For a time I attended classes on meditation. We were given very careful instruction as to technique, rhythm, methods and aims. The classes were held in a beautiful large room overlooking a busy road. Every now and then a bus thundered along; there were many cars, but not enough to give a steady background noise. Learning to meditate under these conditions is difficult, although I'm sure the advanced practitioner takes it all in his stride. I've seen determined Californians select a raving party just to test themselves. Anyway, I tried to cope with all the noises, but was beaten by the noises coming from a garage across the road, where they sold and repaired sports cars. I complained one day, and my instructor smiled at me, and asked, 'You've always wanted a sports car?' It was true, it was the symbol of a stage of my adolescence which I hadn't passed through.

Obviously, we could design a set of symbols for each individual which would categorize all their major centres of attention. But such a set of symbols would require first of all that the person knows and is aware of all major centres of attention; such knowledge is the *result* of using the Tarot (or psychoanalysis) and not the basis. Secondly, these symbols would have to include all major areas of human concern; decisions would have to be made as to where everything fitted. Philosphers of the last three thousand years of recorded history have been trying to do this, and still there is no agreement.

Instead, we do it the other way round. We take a standard set of symbols, and we test our feelings towards these standard symbols.

Now it is possible to see why a standard definition of a standard symbol is not possible; why we cannot say exactly what the cards mean. It is necessary for each and every user to find out his or her *personal* feelings towards those cards. Only when the meanings assigned each card are personal, do the cards become a method of exploring the subconscious.

In the previous chapter I talked about vocabulary, and the way we find out what a given word means, to us and to other people. Now we have to take this a stage further, and start finding out what a given symbol means to us, and to other people.

Most of us start, from very early childhood onwards, finding out the meanings that other people assign to symbols. It is at the stage where the child learns its first words, learns them by watching other people use them and seeing what reaction results, that the 'meaning' of symbols become fixed. The cross becomes that thing on the wall which everyone mentions softly and reverently in one family; in another family every time the word is used, father talks in a very loud and angry voice. The child cannot understand concepts like 'holiness' or 'anti-clericalism' but it learns early on to associate the symbol with approval or disapproval.

At a later date, the adolescent may learn what these words 'really' mean, but the emotional content of the symbol is already fixed; every time the conscious brain hears the word 'cross' it remembers the adult dictionary meaning, but the subconscious hears again father condemning the clergy and their religion. It is the subconscious which gives the symbol its emotional content; this content is based on every event that ever happened in the life of the individual. Some of the events that happened were stories about other individuals and *their* dealings with the symbol. Then again, these stories were told or written by individuals who coloured the story with their own feelings. I can still remember how, at the age of seven, our grade school teacher read us the story of the Crucifixion (it was Easter-time), and broke down in class and sobbed her heart out. We couldn't quite understand about Jesus and his agony, but we could understand the feelings of the teacher about the symbol.

When we grow older, we often rebel against the meanings of symbols. Sons of anti-clericals become priests, children of middle-class professionals become drop-out hippies smoking pot, and sons of the wealthy become Marxists (literally, if you look up the history of the Communist party). They react against the meanings assigned to symbols, and perhaps quite rightly. Some ideas do need some alternative reinterpretation, although of course you must realize this does not apply to any of my ideas – these are all very rational and sane. Nonetheless, ideas and symbols do need critical examination from time to time. But it must be realized that if one meaning of a symbol is rejected, another will be substituted in its stead. And the new meaning is only *another* opinion or feeling. It doesn't represent 'Truth'.

There is a temptation for young people to reject the traditional meanings of a symbol and to examine them anew using a logical or scientific basis. It is almost as if they recapitulated European history. During a very long period, now called the Dark Ages, European man lived by and thought in symbols. The overwhelming majority were unable to write or read; communication was by way of symbols, a custom still remembered vaguely by English inn-signs such as the Rose and Crown, and by the association of green with jealousy. During the Middle Ages, everything had a symbol, and we can still look at paintings from that period to see how far the idea was carried through. The way people were dressed, the materials and colour of their clothes; the way they stand or hold their hands or head; the objects they hold, and how they hold them; all these were signs used to tell important stories about the meaning of the painting.

What was more important, ideas were also bound up with symbols. Very often the idea became the symbol, as for instance the idea that all things revolve round the Earth. There was no way of talking about a new idea, because while you can change ideas, you cannot change symbols.

Then around the end of the fifteenth century, new ideas began to crop up – we call it the Renaissance. It marked the end of the Age of Symbols. People began to read more; gradually printing presses came into being. Ideas began to change, and people become aware that the symbol is not the same as the meaning of the symbol. Slowly the idea that the Earth is not the centre of all things took hold, and people became open to thinking about new meanings to the symbols.

As the years passed by, the wave of new thinking moved to

France, England and Holland. More and more people started rejecting symbols altogether – they wanted totally new symbols which would replace all the old ones. The Revolution in France went the whole hog; after it was all over, people felt it had gone too far, and so they picked up some of the fallen symbols, dusted them off, and hung them up again. But that was only a temporary setback. As we moved on with the times, more and more ancient symbols were rejected. Yet each time we see that the old ones are rejected only to be replaced by new ones. But the new ones lack the slow build-up of association and integration of the old ones; the new use of the symbols last perhaps ten years (think of the swastika, and Hitler's would-be thousand years) and then are lost again.

The height of the anti-symbol rationalist period was the middle and late nineteenth century; the period of Marx and materialism. It was during this period that new ideas began to emerge, with Freud and Jung beginning to demonstrate the one-sidedness of materialist thinking. We are quite accustomed in the twentieth century to accept that basically we are non-rational beings; I think the next step is to accept that we operate in symbols, and have always done so.

If we think of our symbols as being eternal, but our feelings towards or about them, as being personal and liable to change, then I think we have grown through an adolescent stage in our history.

Earlier in the book I talked about the lack of history in the story of the Tarot cards; here I would like to add that the earliest Tarot cards come from the time when people still worked entirely with symbols, i.e. the late Middle Ages. It is more than likely that all the traditional symbols on the cards were so many signs which could easily be 'read' by their users of *that* period. We have largely lost the internationally agreed vocabulary, and have tried to write down the definitions, when in fact they are written on the card itself. But don't forget that the things written on the card were only the designer's opinion as to the meaning of the card. They were not the 'real' meaning, which remains for you to discover, each person for themselves.

How do we discover the meaning a symbol has for us personally? Many books carry the suggestion that we put each card, one at a time, under our pillow before going to bed, and see what dreams we have, and what we feel the next morning. Other people suggest that we meditate on each card. This may be fine if the user knows how to meditate, but in my experience, meditation is not something we practise till we get it right – it is something which needs training under the guidance of someone who has been trained in turn. Meditation is not something like thinking steadily about one single thing, or just keeping still and not letting your thoughts wander. If you have a teacher, or if you are sure you know how to meditate, then fine, just carry on. Otherwise, continue reading.

Most of us are used to being asked to write down the definition of a given word. We get whole lists of words while we are still at school, to write down the meaning, or to translate into French. We complete the task by using another word, or words, to express what we have been taught is the meaning.The teacher marks it right (or wrong), and we go on to bigger and longer words, happy and secure in our belief (and the teacher's) that we 'understand' the word.

But supposing we take a word like 'generous'; if we were asked to give a definition, we might say it means always giving a lot to other people, letting them have a lot. Fair enough, but now try to define 'indulgent'; it also means letting other people have a lot. Oh, well they are really quite different, one means . . . eh. Suddenly we realize that although we can give dictionary definitions to words, which are accurate, we have no real idea as to what they mean, either to others or to ourselves.

It is the same with symbols. We can talk about the meaning of a given symbol, and set down some ideas about it. If we are then asked to do the same for a different but similar symbol, we begin to see that things are less simple. In practice we may be confused when we read the meanings attached to pairs of cards like Temperance and Strength, or Temperance and Justice. It may be easy to explain why we love a particular girl Susy; on a different occasion we talk enthusiastically about Mary. But try to explain how we love Mary in a different way from Susy – only then do we start learning how we really love them.

If we now realize that there is no 'correct' meaning to a symbol, and that we have not enough self-knowledge to state our own ideas, then we must use a third method, one we have already tried with words in the Dictionary Game of the last chapter. We can now start our wallpaper chart.

THE WALLPAPER CHART

We begin by finding an enormous piece of paper; if you think of
something like a newspaper laid out flat, and then half as long again.
You may have to stick several pieces of paper together; stick them
together on the back, since you will need to write on the front. The
finished size will be about one by two-and-a-half metres, or three by
five feet.

You now begin to rule horizontal lines. The first line will be about
an inch below the top of the paper (2½ cm.) and from there you rule
lines about every three inches (7½ cm.) till you get to the bottom of
the page. Next you rule vertical ones. The first vertical line will be
about an inch (2½ cm.) from the left-hand edge, and then you divide
the remainder of the space into twenty-two equal widths. It should
look something like this:

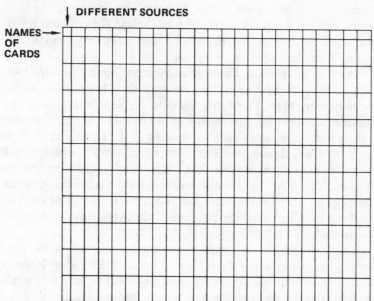

At the top of each column, you mark the name of a card in the Major
Arcana.

The next stage is to borrow or buy books on the Tarot, and read
thoroughly the meanings given to each card of the Major Arcana. If

they give only a few meanings to each card, or just a short sentence, copy it out directly into your chart. Often, however, a whole chapter will be devoted to each card. Then you must make notes, and try to find out what are the most important ideas that the author gives.

In the extreme left-hand side of each row in the chart, you make a note of the book, author, date on which you read the book. Then go along the row, and fill in the ideas about each card under the appropriate heading.

Each book will be read, and the ideas noted on your chart, spread out along the row. After you have read five or six books, give it a rest, and wait for a really rainy day, when you have time and won't be interrupted.

Look at the chart, and read out all the different interpretations you have read in different books. Try to find out what they have in common. Try to reduce all the different ideas to some common ideas, and put the result in the next box below. Do the same for all the cards. Take your time, there is no hurry. You may need several evenings or days for this.

Leave it for a while, and read some more books, perhaps two. Note down any *new* ideas they have; if they have ideas you've already seen, leave them. As you read the new book, check the meanings against the existing list of the first five books. The next time a rainy day comes up, start looking at the boxes you filled in with what you thought were the things that were common. Check them horizontally with other cards, to see that there are no clashes. You can't have two different cards which both contain the attribute 'justice' or 'love'. Either they are two different kinds of love, or perhaps only one card should contain the word 'love'; you must choose which.

The 'reconciled' condensed meanings are entered in the next empty row. By now you should have a good working knowledge of what the cards mean; you should be using them on all your friends and family. As you use them, you will find in practice that the meaning you attach to each card will change over the months, and over the years. Use the remaining rows to record the changed ideas.

One of the most remarkable experiences encountered in reading the Tarot is to discover new meanings 'in a flash' as you use the cards. The learning process using the chart will in fact go on for the rest of your life. In a sense, we can speak of reading the Tarot as a form of meditation, in so far as the reader excludes 'logical' and 'rational' worldly inputs in order to open up the mind to 'other-worldly' energies. Perhaps this sounds a little mystical, but after some years of both meditating and using the cards, this is the only conclusion I have come to.

Chapter 8

TYPICAL PERSONAL CARD MEANINGS

Having talked so long and so feelingly about the lack of meaning in giving out long lists of the precise qualities of the various cards, I am now going to disappoint all those of my readers who expect unwavering integrity, i.e. I am about to issue such a list. But first I shall explain why.

Firstly, as was discussed in the previous chapter, it is necessary to build up a vocabulary by reading and comparing a fair number of other people's vocabularies. As long as it is understood that the list is not an authoritative one, then reading another person's ideas may well prove to be very fruitful.

I am going to begin with the Major Arcana. This is the area with the most profound meanings, and it is also the hardest range to understand, to make one's own. In my own case, I started by memorizing the Major Arcana; it took me something like six months to get a working knowledge sufficient to be able to use the cards, but then I have a bad memory. The Minor Arcana, by way of contrast, took me only a week. A major part of the difference comes from a fact which was not being discussed in the books on the subject then at my disposal, namely that only with understanding do the cards become one's own. And the Major Arcana is much more difficult to understand.

One of the more interesting aspects of human beings is their ability to remember only after they understand. A computer or a memory-perfect idiot can take in things and repeat them word for word. You can train a dog to salivate when a bell is rung, the classic reflex so well demonstrated by Pavlov. You can do the same thing with a human being, and this happens all the time, and not just to prisoners-of-war. But the ability to *understand* comes only to human beings, and then only to their higher centres of experience. Once you understand something, there is little danger of forgetting it. I may well forget the capital of Bolivia, or the date of the Diet of Worms; but once I have understood the difference in essence between the Empress and the High Priestess, I won't confuse the two ladies.

The process of understanding is individual and each person must make his or her own pilgrimage. The journey is exciting, there may be fellow travellers on the way with interesting stories, and occasionally one comes up against a sign-post or a barrier; the final goal is something each pilgrim must reach on his own. The following pages are some of the stories I can tell about my pilgrimage. They apply only to my journey, and I emphasize again, you must find your own unique path.

The twenty-two cards which follow are *my* Major Arcana. As I grew to understand them better and they became more personalized, each card came to have a meaning which is unique to myself. This personalized meaning I will put down in words, but in so doing I will be creating an image which will depart in some way or another from the images which other people hold of the card. In some instances my meaning will be very different, in others only the emphasis will change. In order to *show* the difference such a personalized vision gives, I collaborated with an artist with whom I have a very close contact in producing a series of drawings of the cards. These drawings give a visual image of my feelings towards the cards in so far as I was able to describe these to the artist. Because of our close contact, in some ways the artist was able to capture unspoken ideas from my subconscious in order to create an even more accurate image. So both the drawings and the descriptions that follow are the visualization of one person's feelings concerning the attributes of the cards. You are very welcome to use them, but in no way are they to be regarded as authentic, traditional, accurate or universal. Disregard this small print at your peril.

* * *

THE FOOL

The Fool is the wisest idiot in Christendom. He is unable to take things seriously that other people take seriously, because he sees the petty-minded blindness in such matters. He takes seriously things that other people regard as unimportant. He is someone who does not feel that a fixed home or outlook is necessary, and who travels in hope. I see him as a person who has set off on a new path, not because he knows where it is going, but because he wants to go further than the village where he was born.

Look at him. He has a Jester's cap, and he probably earns the odd meal or night's rest by entertaining the bourgeois in their own homes. But the next day he travels on – jesting for a salary is not for him. He carries his possessions in his little bag – he still feels the need for a few reassuring beliefs and old ideas, even though he has cut off most of them. In his hand he carries a rose, the symbol of love. We cannot see anybody whom he loves, so we can guess that he just has a lot of love in his heart, enough love to care for any person or creature he meets on the way. He is strong enough to be able to love without needing to be loved in return. The rose is held, almost magically, at the tip of his fingers. Here we get another glimpse of an aspect of the Fool – his almost supernatural ability to produce what seem magical effects. The Fool doesn't work hard, or scheme, or trick people, or gamble, or any of the other things that people do in ordinary life in order to get what they want. The Fool says or does the right thing at the right moment, and not until then, to procure all the things that are necessary.

The Fool has an old patched pair of trousers and shoes which are coming apart. He doesn't care enough to be particularly unhappy; if he needs another pair of shoes or trousers, they will turn up in good time. People worry too much about appearances, comfort and security – these things are not for the Fool. So perhaps one day he gets caught out and freezes to death in a snow storm, but until that day he has a carefree existence. He doesn't have to look after his clothes, or send them to the dry-cleaners.

The Fool is walking, he is going somewhere. I don't know where, and neither does he; but he isn't standing still, his Soul is aware that we don't reach perfection by standing still. Lastly, there is no background to the drawing. The Fool just exists in a space all of his own, being his own self without any visible means of support. He is accompanied by a cat, one of the most independent creatures that ever shared this world with Man. The cat likes the company of the Fool as long as the cat is not on a lead, and as long as the Fool doesn't become trapped. As soon as the Fool 'settles down' then the cat is off into the wilderness to lead an exciting existence in the present.

I feel the Fool stands for magical abilities in people, for the part of them that is not trapped by responsibility, taxes and life insurance. It is the part which is in touch with their own potential or with God, if you like. Call it Soul, or a Sense of Humour; it is the bit which makes jokes in a concentration camp, it is the innocence of a small child who wants to be a bus conductor. Picasso is said to have wished to be able to draw like a small child. The Fool stands for people who have cast off the conventions of their peer-group (and that applies just as much to 'Flower-People' as to stockbrokers in the City); they don't know where they are going, but they don't want to stay where they were.

THE MAGICIAN

Here is the medicine man, with his snake-oil, his veritable Elixir, infallible against measles, gout, old age and pregnancy. He comes and gathers a crowd with his arresting clothes and travelling dispensary; he bamboozles them with jokes and fast talking, and eventually, despite their innate common sense, members of the crowd buy his medicine. We all love to be fooled.

The Magician brings excitement into our lives, a touch of the exotic. There's an element of the circus in his performance, and small boys are tempted to run away and become cowboys and Indian fighters. The Magician wants us to believe that he's seen more, done more and come into contact with more 'special' people than you or me. His language is strange and wonderful, he tells stories of people he's met and things he's done; we listen with open mouths. He makes us laugh while telling us how he cures Kings and Crowned Heads; we cry as he tells us of cures to angelic little girls. As someone once said, why spoil a good story with facts.

The Magician stands for fast talk and little action; it stands for manipulation, i.e. making people act the way you want them to, using psychology. The Magician also stands for people who have gifts but use them for mundane purposes. This is symbolized by the objects lying on the table in front of the Magician. If you look carefully, you will see a small knife, a cup, a leafy twig and some coins – these are the symbols of the four suits of the Minor Arcana. The point is that the Magician uses them for making money for food, whereas he could use the symbols as a means of reaching understanding of himself and others.

The Magician cheats people, and lies to them. He also plays tricks on people, fools them and generally can be regarded as a small-time crook or confidence trickster. But at the same time he can cheer people up, cure them of illnesses that 'straight', professional doctors cannot cope with, and teach them things about themselves. The lesson may cost them some money, and they may object that they didn't want that particular lesson just then; nonetheless they may well have needed that piece of insight. It may teach them to stay clear of much greater mistakes.

I think the tag-line about the Emperor's new clothes is known to most people, but I suspect far fewer people know the whole story. Very briefly, a confidence trickster talks the Emperor into ordering some very expensive clothes, which are special in that only people with pure, noble blood can see them; if you can't see them then your blood is impure. Nobody is going to admit to such an inability, so everyone has to pretend they admire the clothes. Finally, the Court Fool protests he really can't see them, and eventually the confidence trick is exposed. Well now, in terms of the Tarot, the Magician is the confidence trickster who profits by people's little inadequacies; the Fool is the Court Jester who is willing to look silly, and in the process 'innocently' rubs the lesson home. So finally we realize that we can only be taken in by the Magician if we want to be taken in.

THE HIGH PRIESTESS
Robert Graves in his book, *The White Goddess,* and Sir Hugh Fraser in *The Golden Bough* both described early matriarchal civilizations where the spiritual power lay with a woman; men came and went but the Queen ruled both in Heaven and upon Earth. With the advent of war-like tribes from the North, these early Mediterranean

the fool

1 the magician

3 the empress

2 the high
priestess

civilizations were overrun, and patriarchy became the standard way of organizing the tribe. The Empress represents the Queen who rules the destiny of men in her own right; the High Priestess is the Queen because she is the wife of the King. The High Priestess cannot rule directly, so she guides indirectly to achieve the results which she deems necessary.

The drawing shows a young lady; she could be a virgin, and she certainly has had no children. In fact, I described her to the artist by saying she should smile as if she has just found out she is pregnant but doesn't want to tell anyone as yet. She does smile mysteriously; there is an inner joy. Her dark hair is an indication of her mystic powers, as is the crux ansata which hangs round her neck. She carries a tray on which rests a book, a glass of wine and a small cake. She is offering hospitality, refreshment and knowledge. She sits in a posture which indicates that she is used to meditating, and might well have finished some five minutes ago. To each side, and slightly behind, are two plants which reach for the heavens; these might stand for balanced aspiration.

I feel that the High Priestess stands for the woman who intuitively sees what you need to grow and develop. She provides knowledge, support and food or comfort when you need it, not when you ask for it. Her silence is golden, and her speech is silver. She is the type of woman who will bear children for her husband because she feels he needs the security of having a son to continue his name and to become what he himself failed to be. She will deny herself in order that her man and her children can grow and develop to their full extent.

The crux ansata round her neck is a key to knowledge, the knowledge that also exists in the book she has ready. You need the key to read the book, the food and wine to strengthen you while you learn. She represents the part of a woman that connects directly to the Fool just as the Hierophant represents the same part in a man. You may call it the Anima, the ideal of womanhood. In a woman it is the spiritually developed human (as against animal) parts of herself; in a man it is his ability to find and understand the magic in a woman.

The High Priestess pays for all this by having to deny herself. Often she doesn't get enough attention, sleep, food, money or whatever for herself; she can get bitter or sour because of it. She also doesn't always resolve the conflict between giving and receiving – she knows how to give, but not always how to receive.

THE EMPRESS

The Empress, as I mentioned in the previous card, is the ruler of men. She needs men to father her children because she wants children; the men are only tolerated because they amuse and are useful. If they do not amuse, or become useless, they are discarded. There is a no-nonsense toughness about the Empress.

She is firmly seated on a bench with Lion's feet on the legs (the Lion is the symbol of the Male part of humanity); she has broad thighs and hips, big breasts. She looks luscious and fertile; her body invites lascivious thoughts. The animal passion for propagating the human race shines out. She holds a Horn of Plenty in one hand (or is it the most enormous phallus?) from which she pours thoughtlessly all the goodies of our wants. In the other hand she holds a bunch of keys; she keeps a tight control over her domain, and leaves no doors casually unlocked in her house of goodies.

At her feet plays a small baby; I think it is a little boy. He is faced with more fruit than he could possibly eat, and yet he stretches out his hand for more. The Empress isn't watching him, but continues to pour out more. I like to think she has masses of blonde hair and a skin of peaches and cream. Altogether a tasty bit of alright.

I think the Empress stands for the ability to enjoy life and the good things in it. She stands for fertility, abundance and the mindless production of ever-increasing amounts of consumer goods. The Empress is an empty-headed dolly who knows what she wants, and is going to get it too. Whether it is what she *needs* is another matter.

The Empress is pragmatic, practical, determined. She often stands for something that is too big to tackle, like a mountain or a bureaucrat determined to go by the form. She is like Mother Nature – 'I ain't asking you, I's telling you.' You have to go round her, or give up, or simply ignore her and let her have her way – the original immovable object.

The Empress isn't interested in what people around her need. She gives or takes away according to what she decides is right. In the old matriarchal societies she married the King for a year, and decreed his death after one year so that his body could symbolically (and actually) fertilize the soil. It was for the good of the tribe – the good of the man chosen to be King for the year simply didn't enter into it. The Empress simply doesn't care about individuals, though she may be concerned about the tribe, or the family. That is, if she is intelligent. If she isn't, she'll simply be in it for what she can get out of it, the archetypal gold-digger.

THE EMPEROR

He sits, four-square and solid. He is the owner and manager of a very large hotel, which he runs as efficiently as possible. He is head of a staff of many servants, cooks, bottlewashers, ostlers, butlers and boot-boys. He has 2,000 table cloths, twice as many sheets, 110 rooms and a banqueting hall. And he manages them all with a firm hand.

His secret is being organized. There is a firm structure of people giving orders and taking orders. Nothing is left to individual initiative unless a deliberate point is made of allowing room for such liberty. Lights are switched off, cutlery is washed and polished carefully, and staff are selected carefully and used so as to make maximum use of their talents in furthering the organization. At the top of the organization sits the Emperor; someone has to be at the top.

He is, of course, very paternalistic, even authoritarian. Individuals, with their tender consciences and weaknesses, are ruthlessly cut out if they do not fit into the organization. Perhaps you don't like him, but remember the alternative, where each does as the mood takes him, can be just as bad. There are some things which can be handled much better by the Emperor. 'Render unto Caesar what is Caesar's, and unto God what is God's' cuts both ways; in order to feed the five thousand on three loaves and five fishes, someone had to sort out the distribution.

So when you see the Emperor, think about order, regularity, structure, organization, paternalism and authoritarianism. It is the stifling of initiative and spontaneity, but it also allows a framework within which new ideas can grow without being swamped in a morass of verbiage.

4 the emperor

5 the hierophant

6 the lovers

7 the chariot

THE HIEROPHANT

The Hierophant is either a brother of the High Priestess, or else they have a very platonic relationship. He also carries the Crux Ansata of eternal life and a book of knowledge. He is in the act of blessing two young people who are perhaps kneeling in front of him.

The Hierophant also rules people, like the Emperor. But he tries to rule them through their heart; his advice or counsel can be disregarded without bringing his wrath on to the sinner. Advance of a spiritual nature is what he offers; this cannot be measured or proven, it depends purely on trust.

Eventually, all people who desire to advance will meet the Hierophant, and must then choose whether to accept and make use of his advice, or whether to reject it and travel at random. The Hierophant loves people, all people, including the sinners and the scoffers, but he cannot help them unless they allow themselves to be helped.

Essentially, he is a lonely man. There are too few people on the same level as himself; the rest of the world either admires him or ignores him. In order to stay stable, the Hierophant must have very large inner resources.

His reward comes from the growth in people who have made use of his advice. Sometimes this may mean that he has to wait a long time for such a reward, and that he has to be patient meanwhile. It can also mean that much of his work will be unrewarded. So an element of selflessness, of altruism, has to be present.

When I see this card, I look for feelings of selflessness, patience, long-term investment, considered advice; higher ideals rather than immediate rewards. It may also be a reference to a woman's ideal lover, or to a man's ideal hero.

THE LOVERS

A young man stands between two ladies, holding an apple behind his back. The lady to his left (nearest to his heart) is pretty, wears simple clothing and smiles sweetly at the young man. The lady to his right (nearest to the place most men wear their wallet) is richly dressed, not as pretty, and is watching her competitor. The young man has to choose to which young lady he will give the apple; overhead flies a little Cupid waiting impatiently to shoot his arrow.

The whole scene reminds me of an observation I have frequently made when walking along the street in the company of any member of the opposite sex (not just wife, girl-friend or fiancée). If, as we walked along, we met another couple going along the opposite way, the man would look at my partner, being attracted to the opposite sex and being interested in all manifestations of the divine form. The woman, on the other hand, would almost invariably look at the other woman; my guess was that she was interested in the competition, since she had already found her man. It seemed almost as if only unaccompanied females ever look at the male half of a couple, much to the annoyance of the female half. But I digress.

The man has to choose between his heart and his wallet, between his feelings and the practical needs of the world. Obviously, we see him at a very dramatic moment, but in fact such a choice has to be made at all times, even in such matters as to whether to go on putting up with things as they are, or whether to throw it all away, and take to the path of the Fool.

When I see this card, I think of choice, and the need to choose; of morals, ethics, life-styles and our decisions based on these philosophies. Perhaps, if you have the time, you may read a book by Oliver Wendell Holmes called *The Autocrat at the Breakfast Table*; somewhere in the middle is a whole discussion of this choice between 'absolute' truth and the conveniences of the world. It is a little too long to put down here, but after all, I have written this book in the hope of stimulating you to look aound. *Verb. sap.* as they used to say.

THE CHARIOT

See the conquering hero ride in triumph; his mighty chariot drawn by two noble steeds, his armour glittering in the sun. We all have dreams of a triumph in Roman style as we ride through the streets celebrating the end of a successful campaign.

Many Eastern philosophies liken Man to a traveller who must travel from one inn across the desert to another inn before it gets dark. The traveller rides in a coach-and-four, driven by a coachman. The analogy represents Man living from birth to death; the coach represents his body, the horses his emotions, and the driver his intellect. The traveller is the Soul, and can only reach his destination if coach, horses and driver (body, emotions and intellect) all work properly.

The general can only come home from a successful campaign if he plans his strategy and tactics intelligently, has adequate materials and seasoned troops, and doesn't let his blood-thirsty emotions run riot. If any one of these is deficient in quantity or quality, then he stands a good chance of being defeated.

Similarly, if the traveller's body is badly diseased or crippled, then extraordinary efforts from the horses and the driver are required to get the traveller home. How many bitter cripples and dwarfs have we not met, people with only average emotional and intellectual talents which could only barely cope with all the problems in this world of able-bodied people. Similarly, people of limited intellect will have difficulty in understanding the complexities of this world and the subtle possibilities of the next. They are not excluded, it is just that much more difficult.

Another way of looking at the picture is to think of people who attach too much importance to intellect or to the body. Mindless athletes and overweight high-brows both represent people who limit themselves.

But both body and intellect represent parts of us which are given at birth. We can bury our talents, or make use of them, but the absolute limit is laid down for us. It is different with emotions. Here we are dealing with behaviour. As an analogy, think of a tin of blue paint. We use the word 'blue' to describe the colour – that is an intellectual decision. Someone with more intelligence might describe it as grey-blue, or blue toned down with orange, or as B.S.1972:4800 18D43 (an architectural standard colour) or even specify it in terms of Angstrom units (the wave-length of the colour measured in one-hundred-millionths of a millimeter). How the paint is made, using plastics, oil, pigments, chemical additives etc. so as to reach paint which will not run, fade, drip, or smell, and which will dry, resist chipping and last the lifetime of your house; those are the body. But its blueness, the *feeling* we get when we see it, is like emotion. The impact that blue has on our senses is emotional; it is not measurable and is inherent in every blue object.

The only decision we can make *vis-à-vis* our emotions is whether we enjoy them, make use of them, let them enhance our lives, or whether we let them rule us.

If we look again at the picture, we see the two goats, very capricious (the word comes from the Latin word for goat) animals, each of which is tending to go its own way. Should the young driver lose control over these goats, his emotions will decide where his war-cart will end up. Perhaps the goats will behave so crazily that the cart will turn upside down.

When I see this card, I feel the emotions are controlling the life of the Querent or that the issue is one of conflicting emotions. Sometimes the emotions are suppressed too heavily, and are rarin' to get out, or are threatening to blow up. But whatever is the external 'mask' the Querent puts on, check to see if there is a balance between body, intellect and emotions. Only when they all put together can the traveller pass on successfully to his goal.

JUSTICE

Justice is traditionally depicted as a young lady with a sword in one hand, scales in the other, and her eyes are blindfolded. On Tarot cards, the blindfold is left off. I think that is because Justice has to see the effect of her pure acts. It is all well and good sending a young man to prison because he has robbed an old lady of her money; but does it help the old lady, the young man or society in general? Only by *seeing* the effects can justice actually *serve* the community, and after all, that is what justice is all about. Justice is only a mechanism to find a happy medium between the boundless desires of the individual and the general good of society. If you suppress the desires of the individual entirely you get unhappy people unable to contribute to the good of the society; if you allow free rein to the desires of the individual, you get a society totally devoted to power, and the consequent reign of sadism and violence prevents the powerless individual from contributing to the good of society. The Comte de Sade (from whom we get our word 'sadism') spent much of his life writing books describing the effects of organizing a society without limits; it was his way of protesting at the society he lived in which seemed to him to be well on the way to becoming a society where justice ignored the effects of the law.

If Justice is not blindfolded, then Justice must see the consequences of her actions. This is what I feel the card is trying to tell me.

So when I see Justice, I think of responsibility, accepting the consequences of our own actions. I also think of guilt, the guilt we feel, or are made to feel by other people, that is caused by feeling that we are responsible for the actions which resulted in these wrong results, results for which we take the blame. Responsibility and guilt are two sides of the same coin, a good instance of the pointlessness of giving different meanings to a card depending on whether it is turned the right way up or upside down. When things go well, we take pride in our ability to take on responsibility; when things go badly, we wallow in our guilt. Many people like feeling guilty, and many other people like being made to feel guilty; after all, it is better than being ignored, isn't it?

Justice wears a sword, to symbolize her need to make decisions, to fight for what is right. She doesn't take scales with her for her long journey, since the 'right-ness' of any decision cannot be judged by weighing the goodness and the badness. But next to her she holds a small trusting child, to remind her of her responsibilities and also of the consequences her decisions will have later on, when the child is grown-up.

THE HERMIT

The Hermit is an old man, a little infirm of body, whose eye-sight is failing. He is in the middle of a very large forest and is trying to find his way out. As it is night, he carries a candle to help him see the way.

Many people start travelling, like the Fool. Perhaps they've heard of the Fool, and also want to be Romantic Travellers. So they pull on stout sandals, a thick coat, and carry a sensible haversack. They prepare themselves adequately for a long journey. As they are convinced that they are old and infirm, they stick to paths they can see, paths which are there to see because so many other pilgrims have trodden them. They do not stop to think that these paths are worn precisely because each successive pilgrim has followed in the footsteps of the previous, and in the process has made (or at least maintained) the path. Eventually the path leads into the forest, deeper and deeper, and the Hermit cannot find his way out. If only he had the courage to get off the path, wade through the old leaves and brambles; he'd stand a good chance of coming to open ground, perhaps even a small village where he could rest and eat. But no, the

8 justice

9 the hermit

10 the wheel

11 strength

Hermit only feels safe on the path, and sticks to it religiously. The candle symbolizes the little bit of the Truth he has found, the part of some or other Religion or Philosophy he has grasped, and which he only uses to follow the path.

This card seems to me about people who daren't jump outside their known and safe ideas. Often they are people who have found a little bit of the truth, and stick to it tenaciously; perhaps a scientist who refuses to believe in Souls, or perhaps a Catholic who believes that all unbaptized people will go to Hell (before I get shot down, not all scientists or Catholics believe these ideas). But is the scientist willing to try to understand mysticism? Is the Catholic willing to believe in the goodness of an Atheist? Hermits have found a bit of the truth, and are sticking to it through thick and thin. So the card suggests obstinacy, tenaciousness, persistence, narrowmindness, fear of the unknown. It also suggests people who feel lost, lack a guide-line and cannot cope with the complexities of this world. They need help, but will often fight offers of help. Make sure they know where you are to be found when they finally learn to accept help and learn to jump off the beaten track.

THE WHEEL

Sometimes we arrive at a time of life when we begin to feel that life is just happenstance; it goes on and on, season after season. The opposite attitude is when we see life as a progression starting at birth, and finishing at our death. Which is right?

Well, perhaps it can be both at the same time. As individuals we experience birth and death, and some sort of progression in between. But an outsider could just as easily say that life on this earth goes on and on. If we use the analogy of a merry-go-round, we see how both images can be true.

At the fair there is a merry-go-round which never stops. The horses go up and down, and the whole merry-go-round turns slowly enough for you to run, jump to get on, and scramble up the moving horse. After you pay your money, you get a ride of five minutes or so; sometimes the owner forgets to make sure you get off at exactly the right moment, but eventually he remembers. Other people get pulled off too quickly or actually fall off. Not everyone enjoys the ride, sometimes the horse's saddle has pins stuck into it, and other people complain because the music from the Calliope is too loud.

Part of the attraction is a ring hanging on a rope. If you lean right over, and time your movements right, you might grab the ring; you then win a prize. What the prize is you will find out only after you have got hold of it. It might be fame, or money, but it also can be notoriety. Some people fall off the horse as they try to reach the ring; other people pull a muscle, and clutch the ring in tremendous pain. This analogy applies to you who are reading it, to me who is writing it, as well as all the other people.

So this card tells me about people who are drifting along without exerting themselves, letting the stream of life carry them. It also applies to people who try too hard, and who gain the whole world and lose their soul (thirty years of constant perusal of way-side pulpits have done their work). Really, the card is about the purpose, or lack of purpose, that people see in their lives. Sometimes I ask them gently whether life should have a purpose. That gets us talking for a long time, and if both of us have not too many preconceptions, we might both learn something. But if we think about the ring too much, we will be like the boy who is told that if he sees a white horse pass, and can avoid thinking of the tail, he will become a very rich man. Which of us, having once heard that story, can avoid thinking of the tail when we see the white horse pass? That's why we're poor, and not just with regards to money.

STRENGTH

My dictionary tells me that Strength is the quality, condition or degree, of being strong. It is, in other words, not brute force. Strength implies the intelligent use of force to achieve a purpose, the use of intelligence being necessary because there is only a limited amount of force available.

A journalist once likened some person to being as ineffectual as Nureyev (a noted male ballet-dancer, just in case you're reading this book in 2078 A.D.) in a rugby match. In fact, the muscles of a professional dancer are probably stronger than a rugby player's and his effectual control over where his body lands up is much greater, since he practises such control day in day out.

I see Strength as a matter of dynamic balance, a phrase which sounds like one of those groovy terms used by a hi-fi manufacturer, or even worse, a corporation dedicated to helping businessmen gain ever more effective control over their personnel and customers. I'll resort to an analogy. Imagine a large tank of water. We pour in the water, and leave it standing. We will ignore evaporation. After a week, the water level will be the same, but green things start floating on the surface, and the whole thing starts to stink. Mosquitoes start to breed; it becomes dangerous. But now imagine that there is a pipe at the bottom of the tank through which water flows to water taps in people's houses; at the top of the tank is a pipe through which water can be added to the system. If as much water is added as is drawn off, then the water level stays steady, but remains sweet and wholesome. Here we have an example of dynamic balance.

Strength in a person exists when that person maintains his equilibrium whatever the pressure from outside. It is easy for any person to be good and sweet-tempered if the people around him are perfect. The real test comes when he has to be reasonable while the world behaves in the unreasonable way we are used to.

The picture shows a man and a woman balanced on one toe each, balancing each other while they carry on juggling. Each of us balances the various parts in us and carries on the difficult act of living. The lion behind them is a symbol of strength; as a child I always loved the lion on the Tate & Lyle (the large British sugar corporation) tins of syrup (I look forward to a free lunch, at least, for that free advertisement) with the bees coming to make a nest in his stomach after his death, and the legend below 'Out of Strength cometh forth Sweetness.' I know that phrase comes originally from the King James' version of the Old Testament, but it is precisely that congruous mingling of Religion and Commerce that demonstrates the quality of symbolism as a non-verbal way, or key, to understanding.

When I find Strength in the cards, I see people balancing, or not balancing, their various abilities and needs; 'keeping their cool' to use a very 'sixties phrase, while all others rush and shout. I see control over the emotions, but also suppression; sometimes people are so determined to control their emotions that they batten down the hatches and the emotions can only get out by making a hole in the side of the ship, thus drowning all. Keep a *dynamic* balance by allowing water to move through your tank; if it doesn't move it will poison you.

THE HANGED MAN

Our sweet, innocent Fool has become 'all hung up'. (I dislike all period phrases, but sometimes they are so apt, one cannot help using them.) He has become attached, by his leg, to the branch of a tree, and hangs till such time as he sees the folly of it all. The real question is, how has he got there? As long as the Fool doesn't get involved, he is free to go on and find out. But should he become attached to some idea or person, then his ability to move freely disappears. Perhaps the Fool, while travelling through the Forest of the Night, met a person who either maliciously, or (more probably) in ignorance, persuaded the Fool to take his place. There are many stories and folk-tales of people condemned to die who persuade another person to take their place. Once the Fool is hung upside down, he becomes the Hanged Man.

At first, the Hanged Man accepts his curious position because he feels he is helping another person. How noble and altruistic. But it doesn't really help anybody; not until the Hanged Man suddenly realizes that there is no real purpose to all this self-sacrifice and noble dedication, can he get away and resume his travels.

When I see this card, I see people who have dedicated themselves and sacrificed their comfort for a purpose; the end justifies the means. These are people trying to help other people for their own good. By only helping other people and sacrificing themselves they will reach to the Kingdom of God. There is earnestness and cold showers, moral dedication and frugality.

The other side of the coin is that people who dedicate themselves have no time to consider what they are dedicating themselves to. The good of other people comes to be more important than growth in themselves. It also becomes very difficult to see things in perspective. Idries Shah, in his book *The Sufis,* has talked about the difference between 'helping' and 'trying to help'. His advice is 'never *try* to help'. If you can help, do so; if you can't, leave it alone. The Hanged Man is primarily about people who believe that 'helping' is more important than the person being 'helped'.

DEATH

In most Tarot packs, Death is depicted as a skellington (sic) mowing a harvest of human heads, hands and feet. Rather gruesome; most

12
the hanged man

13 death

14 temperance

15 the devil

books then go on to emphasize that Death is not about medical terminology, but about change. So that is what I asked the artist to draw.

The two children are enjoying the rose-bush growing on their father's grave. Why not? After all, if older people didn't die, there would be no room for young people. Symbolical of the fact that if we don't stop our old habits and ideas, we are not open to new ideas and ways of looking at things.

You may also note that the name on the tombstone is that of John Barleycorn. John Barleycorn had to be killed, his body hacked to pieces and buried so as to fertilize the ground and ensure the next crop of wheat or barley. Robert Graves has written a book called *The White Goddess* which discusses this concept in exhaustive and poetic detail. Just for now we can note the relationships between life and death, between change and death and between continuity and death.

This card tells me about people to whom change is important, people contemplating a real, abrupt and total change in their lives, their way of thinking. You have to stop believing that all people are out to get you before you can begin to trust people. It is not a change of people's behaviour, but a change in the way we look at people. We stop noticing all the nasty things people do to each other, and instead look at all the kindness and goodness which is expressed each day.

TEMPERANCE

Whether we have just put in five hours in the cold and sleet of a building site or market, or whether we have spent five hours chained to a desk shuffling papers, there is nothing like a good cup of tea. If the tea-lady is saucy, full of rude wit, and smiles at us, we feel suddenly the humanity we all share whether we be brickies, bureaucrats or tea-ladies. That's her gift. We feel revitalized, we suddenly feel we can put in another hour or two on what is essentially a boring, thankless job. Her favourite phrase is 'a little bit of what you fancy does you good'.

Temperance is the card about compromise, about not pushing things too far. Nothing is so important that it justifies hurting another human being. It is about the milk of human kindness, the

crack in the faceless bureaucratic system that allows a nurse to smile
as she makes your bed in the big white hospital where you have
come to die. You suddenly realize that not everybody is against you;
in fact you might even see that there is some kindness in everybody.
There is a spark of humanity in all of us. Hence the symbol of the
tea-lady; even the biggest most faceless corporation has a tea-lady
who knows us all by name.

THE DEVIL

Once, as an exercise, a group of people were given quantities of
plasticine, and asked to model their particular monster. One par-
ticipant moulded a face of a person, fairly realistically, who smiled
at the world. When he was asked to talk about his monster, he
carefully peeled off the face, to reveal a mask underneath. The mask
beneath was a stylized Greek tragedy mask, rather like the one held
by the left-hand puppet. From a realistic smiling face, to a stylized
unhappy face – what a concept. Everyone nodded wisely to show
they Comprehended, they Understood. Then the tragic mask was
lifted, to reveal a flat round disc the size of the mask above, with no
expression at all. It merely had two round holes roughly where the
eyes would be, and a slit corresponding to the mouth. *That* was his
monster.

People feel they have to behave. They feel they need masks, or
persona, to use the technical phrase of the qualified psychiastrist, in
order to feel dressed and ready to see other people. The mask we
choose depends on the circumstances, and on the role we see
ourselves as playing in relation to the people sharing the scene.
People who first come across this idea very often exclaim indig-
nantly that they don't have a mask, that they are open and honest
and truthful. Watch them explaining the facts of life to their children, or how they came to be exceeding the speed limit. Listen to
them talking to a clergyman, and to a beggar.

Eventually, most people realise that they do have masks. The real
problem is how much they 'identify' with their mask; how much
they believe that the way they behave is real, is true, is honest.

Another area of belief in people is that the way they feel is the
proper reaction to outside stimuli. Do people really feel insanely
jealous when their wife has a brief fling with another man? Are you

totally devastated when your aged mother dies? Many of our concepts on 'proper' behaviour and feelings are derived from the things we read, the plays we see, the films we watch. Very often the very words we use when we express our feelings come straight from some film, book or play.

In the picture I asked the artist to make about the Devil, we see the two puppets carefully holding their masks while trying to pay homage to Bacchus. The Devil is genuinely enjoying life; he is doing what he wants to, without wondering about what he should look like, what he should be doing in order not to antagonize people. The puppets below cling to their little masks.

The Devil is about preconceptions, the beliefs about the world which prevent people from finding out the truth. It is about people who limit themselves; they feel that they can't do something because *they* won't let them, or that they should do something because *they* say one ought to. The most tragic thing about people in the clutches of the Devil is the apparent ease with which other people can see their problems and how to get out of them. Almost like saying to a fat person that all she's got to do is eat less. Think about your own little habits, and how easily you could stop them. Habits like believing that you can help people, that you are more sensible, better organised, have a richer inner life. Other habits like believing that you have to be obsequious to your boss, polite to clergymen and bishops, careful with Granny and small children. Oh yes, not one of us is entirely free of the Devil; but at least we can become aware of our chains.

THE TOWER

This is logically the next card after the Devil. It is about the sense of betrayal we feel when our preconceptions are shattered. Traditionally the card is about a death, a sickness, betrayal, treachery; many fortune-tellers regard it as a card of ill omen. But look at it another way.

All of us feel the need for protection from the cold inhospitality of the world. We build defences of some sort or another. We build a tower, strong enough to withstand rain and storms from the enemy with his arrows and gunpowder. We gain security, but only for a price. That price is our ability to move, to grow, to develop. God looks down, and feels that unless he can get us out of the castle, we will just stay there and stay put. So he sends us messages, gives us opportunities, drops little hints. We see them as temptations, or ignore them. In the end, God realizes there is only one way to get us out of the Tower. He 'zaps' the building with a stroke of lightning, the Tower collapses and we are forced out in the cold. Now comes the moment of real importance.

Will we look at the ruins, bemoan our bad luck, and try to build up the Tower again with the same stones? Or will we realize that this is God's way of saying, 'Get off your fat behind and do some thinking'? The Tower represents the fact that as our illusions are shattered we must grasp the opportunity to grow. That is why I asked the artist to show the Tower as a picture of two children totally engrossed in building their sea-side fort. Only when Reality starts tearing up their picture do the children realize that all is illusion. Will that knowledge drive them insane, or will they grasp the opportunity to make friends with the giant?

So the card is about illusions being shattered. That is why it so often is about death, treachery, illness. When the card appears I see opportunities to be grasped, and illusions about to be shattered, abrupt changes just beyond tomorrow, people and things around the Querent being not what they seem to be. When her husband suddenly runs away with a blonde secretary, will the wife left behind venomously pursue the errant man, or will she apply for a course at the teacher training centre which she always wanted to follow? One cannot tell in advance; only when people are thrown into the deep end of the pool do we find out if they will let themselves drown or struggle to learn to swim.

THE STAR

The Star is about hope and trust. I asked the artist to draw a mermaid as a symbol; perhaps you have read or heard the story of Hans Christian Andersen's mermaid who wanted to become a princess. This undeniably *pure* young lady (she must be a *virgin*, seeing as how the relevant half of her is fish) pours water from two jugs into the sea. Behind her is a rainbow, that symbol of hope and promise (think of the story of Noah and the Ark); the bird singing

16 the tower

17 the star

18 the moon

19 the sun

on the orange tree believes in the joy of Nature after the rainstorm (of course it's after a rain-storm, look at the rainbow). Above all this idyllic picture shines the Star, the focus of our longing for the unattainable goal of perfect happiness. A small bird is bringing her a letter.

I feel the Star is essentially about our identification with the rest of humanity. The sea can stand for the human race if it is seen as a unity; each person is just a drop in the vast ocean. As a mermaid, the lady shows she herself is part of the sea. The water in the two jugs is being poured back into the ocean. Each of us is a clay jug of flesh and bones, in which is poured the water of eternal life. When we die, the water is poured back into the ocean; we only 'borrow' the water of the Soul for the duration of our lives.

I feel that the fact that I belong to the ocean gives me trust, the trust from the phrase: 'This too shall pass'. The bird with the letter is a message from friends saying they love me; just as the rainbow is a message from God to say He loves me.

The Star is also about hope, the hope that things will come out all right. Perhaps in the here and now things aren't going perfectly, but up there the star shines; perfection exists in some place in the sky. We might not be able to get there immediately, or perhaps we might never get there, but eventually we or our children will get there. We must be able to, seeing as the star exists for all to see. So, in a sense, the Star can also stand for our vision of the perfect, the Platonic Ideal.

Of course, people who are too full of trust and hope won't take everyday precautions and care. God cares for those who care for themselves. Some people want to trust, desperately so, because that way they can put off the evil moment. They don't want to face evil, or fight it; by looking only at the positive things in life they miss building up the strength to be able to deal with the negative things.

As a personal image, I always think of Anne Frank in her attic in Amsterdam, recording the life of a girl whose life consisted more of promises than events.

THE MOON
She sits by the water and feels, reflects, ponders. She looks at a reflection of the Moon; the Moon shines with reflected light from

the Sun. In her hand she holds a withered twig. Lovely as she is, I feel she is alone in the night; to quote Fitzgerald, 'In the depth of one's soul it is always four o'clock in the morning'. The combination of robe, long hair and the surrounding gloom make it difficult to guess her exact form.

The Moon is a symbol of femininity, of passive acceptance. The pool of water is a symbol of emotions and feelings. The reflection is a symbol of unreality, disconnection. Her robe is a symbol of mystery. The leafless twig is a symbol of a living thing that either has come to the end of the circle of life, or is just beginning a new one. The Moon is the last of the Trinity of women so well described by Robert Graves in his *The White Goddess*; the High Priestess is the Nymph, the Empress is the fertile Mother, and the Moon is the old Hag or Crone, she who buries the dead.

When I see the Moon card, I think of emotional distance, of alienation; it can be insensitivity, coldness or frigidity. It can be the lowest point in a cycle which rises and falls rhythmically. The Moon is about male submission, inevitability of natural processes. It can be a wet blanket, despair, loneliness and depression. Yet the Moon has a tender heart for all those who genuinely love her – think of her as the Queen of Poetry.

THE SUN

The Head of the Household strides across his land to sow the seed which will grow over the year to feed the rest of the family that stands admiringly at the edge of the field. Above all, a benign sun shines. We feel the happiness and the clarity.

The man is in direct contact with the realities of life. He is sowing the seed which he will reap next year for his bread. Not quite the same as filling in forms to check the rate of growth of the interest rate charged by banks on farmers who need to borrow money to buy tractors with which to pull the plough that actually tills the land. The realities of life stand at the edge of the field, admiring his industry and skill. The man walks over Mother Earth, he is handling the wheat. He feels happy and at peace with himself. He may seem somewhat limited to the sophisticated slickers from the big city, but who is to say what constitutes happiness. Nonetheless, it is true to say that such contentment does prevent the peasant from reaching the limits of his potential. But perhaps that is a small price to pay.

I see the Sun as a card about the need in people for personal happiness, for contentment, for peace and being at one with their surroundings. They seek, or have found, an escape from the pressures around them. Often they are people who believe that somewhere is their personal happiness, and all they've got to do is find it, and hang on to it. Frequently they seek advice through Tarot readings as to where this happiness is to be found in the fond belief that some wiser person can 'see' their place of happiness and tell them the way. I can only tell them that happiness is something you experience, not something you find.

JUDGEMENT

This card is about understanding. I found it very hard to find a way of showing somebody understanding anything. I thought about Archimedes watching the bath overflow, and suddenly jumping out, running across the street, shouting 'Eureka'. No, this didn't feel right. There were numerous other images; finally I hit upon the picture of a little girl watching a caterpillar, and suddenly understanding the relationship between caterpillar, cocoon and butterfly.

You know, all of us walk this earth as caterpillars. We eat voraciously, ruining the earth in the process. Then we die, and only after our death are we transformed to butterflies. Which of us really understands the relationship between before and after? All we can do is talk of Life, Death and Heaven.

Perhaps suddenly the little girl has an insight into her own situation. She has to grow through her own childhood, change into the often ugly aspect of the adolescent before becoming a beautiful butterfly.

So I see Judgement as a card about the insight, or lack of it, that people have into themselves; it is a card about the way they understand their place in the scheme of things, their relation with and to other people.

THE WORLD

Miss World stands on the podium, first prize-winner of the competition, watched by her admiring parents. In the background is painted a crown of laurels.

20 the last
Judgement

21 the world

Miss World doesn't ask questions about the nature of the competition, or its purpose. She is just proud that she has won. So are her parents, although I think they look a tiny bit worried as they watch their darling. Perhaps they are afraid that she will be spoiled by all this success, or perhaps they are worried by the possibility that she will not be able to stand defeat when she competes as a teenager in a stiffer competition. Never mind, she's happy just now.

When I see the World, I think of all the people who compete 'because the prize is there'; because they see other people competing, or because they hear other people talk admiringly of people who have won such a prize. I see the card as being about all the things people do because everyone else does them too, or because the Jones do them, or because Mummy/Daddy always says I ought to do them.

So the card is really about happiness in the eyes of the world. If the way other people see happiness makes you happy too, good luck. But be careful that you do not measure happiness only in terms of other people's approval.

* * *

Those were the cards of the Major Arcana. I think you will realize by now that I see them as illustrations of the illusions we have which prevent us from reaching understanding. Very often we do things for the best of reasons; yet we must realize these reasons are only justifications and that all these good intentions and excuses are only hindrances. That doesn't mean we must become totally selfish and think only about our own development. That is only another illusion, the illusion that by working hard at it, we can further our development, our personal happiness. Perhaps, finally, we realize there is no one way to Nirvana.

Having sauntered slowly through my personal garden of the Major Arcana, we now take a quick gallop through the vegetable garden of the Minor Arcana. Many of my pupils have in the past asked me whether I *ever* used the Minor Arcana, seeing as how I mostly used the Major Arcana in my readings. Well, I must confess that I am more interested in the puppets than in the strings that move them (I am indebted to Richard Gardner for the simile). The Minor Arcana talks about the events that happen to us, whereas the Major Arcana talks about our feelings, our needs and stresses. I am much more interested in people than in the things that happen to them. But that doesn't mean that everyone should take the same attitude. Obviously, some Querents really want to know about future events. Also, some readers want to know about the Minor Arcana. So here it follows.

The Minor Arcana is composed of four suits. These are called Wands, Cups, Swords and Coins. I like to think of them as representing Fire, Water, Air and Earth respectively. Other writers think differently, so please remember, there is no absolute. When I am using the cards in, say, a Pontoon Spread (see chapter 10 for an explanation) then I like to think of these four suits as representing Spirit (or Energy), Emotions, Intellect and Practicality respectively. Let's discuss these in slightly more detail.

Wands
These are usually shown as sticks with buds, leaves or twigs sticking out from each side at intervals. I see them as something that is going to

grow. Perhaps Enthusiasm, perhaps Drive or Determination or Get-Things-Moving. There is a lot of Energy, the feeling that makes people carry on their task in the belief that things will be all right on the night. Wands are tied in with Belief, Hope, Faith, Trust. Think of the Wands as being members of the Sales Department of a large factory; they do a bit of advertising, sales promotion and public relations.

Cups

Think of wine glasses holding the noble liquid that enables us to overcome our inhibitions against showing our feelings. The feelings may not always be nice or genteel or polite, but there they are: both love and hate, passion and indifference. People who don't have emotions are people who suppress them; by keeping them down now they will have to face them later and in a much less honest way.

I think we all have some idea of emotions and what they are; not all of us are clear about why they are necessary and important parts of a human being. If we carry on the analogy started under Wands, we can think of Cups as being the Personnel Department of the company. Funnily enough, many Managing Directors also don't attach much importance to how staff are treated, or, for that matter, customers. As Henry Ford remarked about his precious motor cars, 'You can have any colour as long as it is black'.

Swords

Swords cut, like unkind words. The suit of Swords is about reason, intellect, cleverness, using words rather than deeds; it is about opinions, judgements, attitudes, rationalizations. In our large factory, Swords are the Management, the decision-makers. There is nothing wrong with being a Manager, as long as such a person realizes that he is only a quarter of the whole, no more and no less necessary than all the other quarters.

Coins

Coins (sometimes called Pentacles) are about money, about practicalities. People want to hold things, to know things as being definite. None of this nonsense of ideas, feelings, trends. If you can point to it, or hold it in your hand, then it comes under Coins.

We have landed in the part of the Factory where things are actually made: foremen, skilled artisans, floor-sweepers, machines, assembly belts.

From the above we can see that none of them works without all the others. A factory needs workmen and machines, a management, a personnel department and a sales forces. Miss out any one of them, and you'll get extraordinary trouble; the absence of one may cause trouble sooner than the absence of another, but eventually any missing department will cause the company to go bankrupt. Similarly, a person needs energy and drive, awareness and contact with his emotions, a good intellect and lots of practicality to survive.

Each of these suits is divided into four court cards and ten pip-cards. The four court cards are usually shown as a King, a Queen, a Knight and a Page. But some packs show the Page as a Princess, and for the reasons which follow, I prefer the latter arrangement.

In reading Fraser's *The Golden Bough* (which is very long and repetitious) or Robert Graves' *The White Goddess* (shorter and more interesting, although perhaps less definitive) we are told about a way of life apparently widespread in the Ancient World. Briefly, at the head of the tribe rules a woman who is the personification of a heavenly Goddess. The most important Goddess to our early forebears was the one governing fertility, the fertility of the soil, of the animals kept for food, and of the human members of the tribe. If the soil was fertile, and animals and humans multiplied, the tribe as a whole survived. So what would be more natural than to make the Goddess of Fertility head of them all? And here on Earth she was personified in the person of the head of the tribe. This is our Queen.

Now, despite any apparent anomalies like the ignorant Trobriand Islanders who didn't know the facts of life (I personally think this ignorance was the manifestation of a taboo upon what was 'proper' to confess to knowing), most early peoples that kept or hunted animals knew very well that having babies needs a fertile mother as well as a fertilizing agency, i.e. a father. But they also observed that after fertilization the father doesn't need to stick around. And, at this point, they adopted an analogy with far-reaching consequences. If, they reasoned, the mother is likened to the earth, then as we can see the earth being fertilized by the seed (of corn), we imagine the mother being fertilized by the father. But, after the seed is put in the ground, it is left there and reappears miraculously the next spring. Very well, in that case, whoever fertilizes the Queen also has to be put under the ground. This is exactly what they did; every year the Queen's lover was killed and buried in order to ensure the fertility of the Queen, the soil and the animals and humans in the tribe. So each year the old King dies, and each year a new King is chosen. The new King is chosen from the promising young men of the tribe, very often after a challenge and mortal combat with the old King. You might see the Knight in the Tarot pack as the up-and-coming King.

Lastly, you may ask, what happened to the children of the Queen, and how was the new Queen chosen? In simple terms, her boy children became ordinary citizens of no importance, but one of her Princesses was chosen to be the next Queen.

The above is a very simplified and perhaps not totally accurate picture of the Matriarchal society. However, it is enough to enable you to distinguish between the different Court cards.

The King is a reactionary force, trying to hold on as long as he can to his short-lived reins of power. He can be obstructive, despotic, autocratic, but also kind, magnanimous and noble. He is at the top now, but will shortly die. He resists change, since any change cannot be but for the worse. The Queen is the long-term conservationist force. She doesn't like changes unless they are clearly for the good of the tribe. But once she knows that it is better she will allow change, although she prefers small changes coming about gradually. The Knight is the onrushing force. He wants to become King, and is impatient, headstrong, energetic. Any change is for the better, since he can only go up. He doesn't know or even think about defeat. He wants revolutionary change.

Lastly, there is the Princess or Page. She represents long-term evolutionary change. Eventually she will succeed the present Queen, and hence she is already contemplating some long-term plans that will be put in action when she reigns. Give her time.

Got all that, so far? Good, now we finally can come on to the pip-cards, one to ten. For these I simply use the nearest brand of numerology, calling ten a zero. Here follows a list you may want to use, if you are doubtful or not energetic enough to find your own:

One: A beginning, unity, the individual and manifestation

Two: Reality, duality, togetherness, the masculine principle

Three: Creativity, evolution, the feminine principle

Four: Logic, divisiveness, structure, materialism

Five: Wholeness, humanity, expression; five is the child of two and three

Six: Progress, development, a turn for the better, synergy; six is the product of two and three

Seven: Stands for stability, influence, integrity

Eight: Continuity, completion of a cycle, preparation for dissolving; eight is two raised to the power of three

Nine: Perfection, and rest; nine is three raised by the power of two

Ten (or zero): Potential, energy waiting to be released

Now all these descriptions of the significance of numbers may seem rather vague, so I think the best thing is to show you how I use the system in practice. Suppose I turn up the seven of Wands; the ideas of stability, influence and integrity are applied to the Sales Department of the Factory. Right, I interpret the card to mean that the Querent has nursed an idea or enthusiasm to the point where the Sales Manager 'buys' the idea and starts putting it into practice; it is no longer a crazy or fantastic idea. Similarly, the four of Coins would be read as logic, divisiveness, structure or materialism applied to the Shop Floor of the Factory; I see the card as a case of gross materialism, of letting money rule the heart. And so on. Later, when we discuss the way cards are to be read in spreads, in combination with each other, you will really start appreciating the apparent 'vagueness' of the meanings for the Minor Arcana.

To sum up this very long chapter, I must again emphasize that the above meanings are my personal ones, meanings which I have gradually evolved to suit my personal background. As I grow older, these may change, sometimes slowly, at other times at great speed. In no way are these meanings accurate, or God-givèn; they are not revealed knowledge. The only real way to finding the meanings to the Tarot cards is for you to get in touch with your subconscious and develop your personalized set of meanings. These can make use of other people's ideas, they can crib, borrow, steal; but not one is *right* in the way that can be rewarded by a prize in a quiz. They are only right if you find that they open up new ideas and concepts in your mind. Here endeth the lesson.

part three

Chapter 9

SPREADS IN GENERAL

In the previous section I talked about individual cards; what each means in terms of words and symbols. I discussed ways in which you can find out what these cards mean to you personally, and I set out some of my personal feelings (students of psychoanalysis are asked to refrain from sending me the results of any insight into my character they have obtained from reading that part). Now I am going to talk about the way in which the individual words are put together to form a sentence. These sentences are called spreads.

Perhaps a more accurate analogy would be to call the spreads the grammar of the Tarot. By grammar I mean the formal way in which words are combined to form sentences. Every language has a grammar of one sort or another. Even when we are very small, we are told that 'the cat sits on the mat' is grammatically correct, while 'cat on the mat is sitting' is not. The word order *matters*; I chose those particular examples because in other languages the second one would be more correct than the first.

Grammar involves word order, and the tense of the verb, whether it is past, present or future. It involves deciding on the number of people involved, their sex, whether someone is doing something or whether it is being done to them. The actual words involved can change, but their order remains the same. We can say:

'the cat sat on the mat'
'the cat stood on the mat'
'the cat stood on the table'
'the vase stood on the table'

– notice how we have changed all the words in the sentence without changing the form. Well, that 'form' is really what a spread is about, an arrangement which allows for individual cards to fit into a pre-arranged pattern.

There are many different patterns, just as there are many different ways of arranging a sentence. A little further on I shall talk about each individual spread, but first I'll talk about spreads in general.

Spreads can vary from three cards to the whole 78-card pack. Every book on the subject (and this book is no exception) shows a number of spreads. Usually, the beginner is urged to start with a simple spread and work his or her way to the more complicated. Rather as we start with simple 'the cat sat on the mat' sentences and work gradually to the very complicated, involuted sentences beloved by civil servants and insurance companies.

Straightaway the astute reader will object that the writings of the civil servants and the insurance companies are carefully written so as to cause the maximum amount of confusion together with the minimum amount of information. So it is with spreads. Generally speaking, the fewer cards there are in a spread, the more definite the information – but the more likely that the Reader will get it wrong.

Imagine for a moment that the Querent asks whether there will be good fortune coming his way. You might decide to choose only one card, and say 'Yes' if the card is an even number, and 'No' if uneven. There is no evasiveness or subtlety, but your chances of being right are only 50% – you might as well have tossed a coin.

If you used twenty cards (or words) then you could talk about good luck coming only under certain conditions of the Querent's behaviour, or after other events had passed. There would be less certainty and definition.

It is certainly possible to use complicated and involuted sentences in order to express one's feelings as accurately as possible, but remember for every Henry James there are ten thousand civil servants waffling away.

If you want to express yourself as clearly and yet as interestingly as possible, then until you develop a style of your own, it is best to use reasonably short sentences, with a clear structure. Similarly, when you start using your cards in a spread, pick patterns which are of a reasonable complexity. Reserve the very simple spreads for moments of mystical intuition, and the very complicated spreads for the time when you can make full use of them. Using complicated spreads merely because they are a challenge is rather like making complicated sentences when trying to create a good impression.

Many years ago I replied to an advertisement asking for someone to give English lessons to a Pakistani gentleman who knew some English but who felt he needed to know more in order to master it. It quickly developed that back in Pakistan, where he had learned English in the local secondary school, he was rewarded for learning how to spell and define long complicated English words. There were fewer marks for short English words. Hence he knew words like 'abrogated', although he couldn't use the word in normal conversation. The same applied to his sentence structure, which was complicated, and studded with 'whereas' and 'notwithstanding'; as a result his use of English was difficult to understand at times. I put him on a course of an hour each day watching television or listening to the radio, and then writing short sentences of noun, verb and predicate only. No conditional or other subordinate clauses; I also ruthlessly struck out long and complicated words and asked him to find shorter, more generally used ones.

Right, having talked about the relation between language and the Tarot, I will now talk only about spreads, and stop using analogies. So, you are by now burning to know, how do we arrange a spread?

A number of cards are chosen (how they are chosen is discussed later on in the book) and put down in a pattern. Examples of these patterns follow, but right now we are looking at the *idea* of pattern. Each position in the pattern is given a heading, such as Hopes and Fears or Nearest and Dearest or the Past. Then we can talk about the past, or the hopes and fears of the Querent by looking at the position under which such information is to be found, and describing the attributes of the card occupying that position.

Supposing for instance the position of the Past is occupied by the card called the Lovers, then you might decide (using *my* set of interpretations for convenience) that in the past the Querent has had to choose or make a decision. You don't know what that choice or decision was, but you can tell that it was made at some time in the past.

Other books you will have read on the Tarot (that is, if you are following my ideas in chapter 7) will have set out some interesting spreads. The normal method is to give a diagram showing you the pattern in which they are to be laid out, and then each position is marked with its subject. There will then be a short discussion as to exactly what a phrase like Hopes and Fears means, which will be followed by a pious mention of the fact that adjacent cards will influence the meaning of the given card. The discussion will often, but not always, finish with a fully worked-out example.

Now it is that phrase 'adjacent cards will influence' which really hit me when I first started to study writings on the Tarot. After all, if a book spends three-quarters of its content on describing the meanings of the cards, taken one at a time, and another 24% on showing you the spreads, then it is rather like a dictionary which lists the meanings of all the words in a foreign language, gives you a few typical sentences to show the way of putting these words together, and then casually mentions that the meanings of the words depends on the other words in the sentence! That could cover an awful lot of ground.

So, when we look at spreads, we must describe the pattern, the positions in that pattern and what they are describing, which cards influence which others, what the spread is used for, what effects you can create using it, and finally, which cards you should use in it.

I think the idea of arranging cards in a pattern, and assigning each position a heading is fairly simple. But the idea of cards influencing each other is more complicated. Let's go into some detail, and see how this works in practice.

Suppose I wish to describe a friend of mine. I can begin by saying he is an emotional man, i.e. someone with strong emotions. I use only the one adjective 'emotional' to describe him. This will give you some idea of what the man is like, but not much.

Now if I add a second adjective 'sensitive' to make the phrase 'a sensitive, emotional man' you might get the picture of a person who is easily aware of other people's feelings, and is not afraid to express his own. But suppose that instead of the word 'sensitive' I had used the word 'angry' to obtain the phrase 'an angry, emotional man'. We get a totally different picture; we see a man who is easily angered, or perhaps even is angry all the time, and who has furious rows with other people. You see how the single adjective 'emotional' is changed by the adjective next to it.

Similarly, if in a spread about a person, I saw the Lovers under the heading the Past, all I would know is that there had been a decision or choice made in the past. But if the card next to it were the six of Swords, which usually is taken to mean a journey across the water, then we would know the decision or choice had to be about whether to make such a journey, or perhaps where to go. If, on the other hand, the card next to it were to be Death then the choice or decision had to do with making a drastic change.

Any two adjectives taken together produce a subtle, third meaning which is different if either one of the adjectives is combined with yet another adjective. If you use three adjectives, like *Time Magazine*, to describe someone, it becomes either very subtle, or more usually, meaningless. So in the early stages, read combinations of cards in the spreads two at a time. Later, when you feel more comfortable, use three at a time.

'The problem now arising on platform 3' is how to decide which is the 'adjacent' card. Here I suggest we look at something which is rarely perceived, namely the pattern of the spread itself. It is in fact a puzzle as to why the cards have to be arranged in patterns which make pretty geometric patterns, but seem to have no other function.

Laying the cards in a row, and designating headings by saying the first one is about your character, the second about your nearest and dearest, and so on to the end of the row, seems to be an exception. Most spreads use complicated patterns like the cross, a circle, a horse-shoe, the tree of life, and the like. Why? If we look at a painting of any time between the Renaissance and the Impressionists, we will notice the attention that is paid to the positioning of the objects or people in the picture. Very often the artist takes the trouble to arrange objects in such a way that the eye is led to a particular object or person which forms the subject of the painting. There are certain tricks or rules which can be used to achieve this, and part of an artist's training is to learn how to make use of these.

Similarly, the pattern in a spread is designed to lead the mind from certain positions to certain others. This rarely follows the order in which the cards are laid, but seems to follow rules which are based on the way the human brain coupled to the human eye perceive movements and relationships that are significant. Some of these rules of perception form the basis of the study of the psychology of perception; it is only recently that scientists began to set out formal rules and discover relationships which have formed the basis of human activities and until now were formulated on a purely intuitive basis. A concrete example will be shown in chapter 11 – the Celtic Cross.

For the present, it is enough to realize that each time we use a spread, we must try to discover which cards are adjacent. I have set out some of these patterns of adjacency in detail in the chapters on individual spreads, but it must be observed that adjacency, generally speaking, is through association of ideas and subject, rather than the fact that cards lie near each other. Deciding which cards are 'adjacent' is part of the reading; there are rules you can use that will give you relationships which apply to most readings, but just as the great artist learns to ignore or break the rules, so must you learn to break the standard patterns. If you learn the rules first, then later, with experience, you will learn how and when to break them.

At this stage, before you settle down to read about the individual spreads, you may be wondering about the need for all these different patterns. As already explained, this is partly due to the need for greater or lesser detail, subtlety and accuracy. The other reason is that we need different spreads to answer the many different questions that arise.

The Querent may ask you to give the answer, yes or no, to a specific problem; he doesn't want to know when or why, just yes or no. Another Querent isn't quite sure what the problem is, and asks for clarification, whilst a third is debating a choice, and would like guidance. Each needs a different spread, the spread being designed to throw light on the problem rather than just tell us something which we might not feel the need to know. Someone with a broken arm doesn't need a general health check-up, he needs a splint. Only after the broken arm is set can the doctor start asking about the general health of the patient.

The final point to bear in mind when choosing a spread is the choice of cards. By this I mean that it is not always necessary to use the full pack of 78 cards, nor even always desirable.

The pack is sold as a set of 78 cards, but in fact, even the beginner will realize that it can be readily divided into a Major and a Minor Arcana. Furthermore, the Minor can be divided into four suits. It is perfectly possible to use only selected parts of the pack for specific purposes.

For instance, as I have shown, the Major Arcana is a much 'deeper' psychologically or mystically oriented series, whereas the Minor Arcana is more about the everyday *events* that occur. In everyday practice, this means that when you want to simply tell fortunes, it is useful to use only the Minor; when someone needs to make an important decision about what for want of a better phrase I will call 'life style', or is in deep trouble, then we use only the Major. If someone needs a specific answer to a money or job problem, use only the suit of Pentacles; if they need to know about their loved ones and friends, use the suit of Cups.

I think that about covers the use of spreads in general, and the time has come to start looking at individual spreads. It would be useful to read all the spreads right through, so that you can pick up some of the ideas, and then try a simple spread and get used to it.

Chapter 10

LINEAR SPREADS

I shall start with the simplest spreads, which can be grouped together under the heading of linear spreads. They all consist of choosing a number of cards, which, either singly or in groups of three, are set down next to each other in a horizontal line. Each card, or group of three cards, is given a heading, and the Reader starts at the left, and works his way to the final card on the right. Later on, in chapter 18, I shall go into much greater detail on the method of choosing cards, but at this stage it is sufficient to say that the pack (or parts of it) are shuffled by the Reader, after which the Querent selects the required number and hands them over to the Reader. The Reader then sets them out in the required pattern, and starts reading out whatever he sees in the cards.

First of all, let's take the very simplest sort of spread. I've decided to call it the three-card trick. We ask the Querent to choose three cards (obviously without looking at the face of the card) and hand them to us. The first card is put down on the table, face up, and this card tells us about an *event* that will happen to the Querent. We cannot say exactly when it will happen; all we know is that it *will* happen – it isn't something that has already happened. If the card should be the two of Cups, then we predict a marriage or, in this enlightened age, perhaps a love affair without holy sanction or even a municipal councillor's official blessing. If the card should be the Page of Cups, perhaps we can predict a happy event such as a baby, or the offer of a much-wanted job that starts a career. The three of Swords would mean a bitter quarrel, whereas the Lovers would mean a decision. Obviously, each of these cards has many meanings; it is up to you to select the one you *feel* is right.

At this stage many people look up with a hurt, betrayed feeling.

'How will I know which meaning is the right one?' they will wail. 'We have come here to learn how to choose the right one, and at this stage you abandon us, and tell us to choose, without telling us how.' Here I can only say that *any* choice you make is the right one. Just choose whichever you feel is right; the working of your subconscious will make sure it is the right one. As long as you don't defend your choice by using any form of logic, it will be all right. It is precisely the permission to make illogical choices in guessing truth that is the requisite 'power' of the Tarot.

When you have described *what* is going to happen (one sentence or even a phrase, is enough at this stage) you turn over the second card, face up, and put it to the right of the first. That card tells us what the Querent will *feel* about the event. If the first card is for instance the Page of Cups (and we guessed a baby is on the way) then should the next card be the ten of Rods which indicates the feeling of being burdened, then we can say that the lucky lady is perhaps ill-prepared, it being the first one of the family. Alternatively, it can be the ninth baby, in which case it will be a burden. If we take a totally different example where the first card is the three of Swords, indicating a violent quarrel, and the second card is the five of Cups, indicating a sense of loss over the spilling of the cups of happiness, again we have a predicted incident coupled to the Querent's *feelings* about that event.

Lastly, the third card is turned up, to show what the Querent will *do* about it. In the first example of the previous paragraph, the third card might be the Queen of Rods, who is a loving and warm woman; we can predict that the prospective mother will love the baby and look after it in the hope that it will grow into someone who will make it all worthwhile. In the second example, the third card might be Temperance, indicating the making of a compromise. Perhaps we can guess that the compromise is made because the friendship is more important than the quarrel.

Once we have laid down the third card, and talked about it, we are then free to try to see the three cards as a unity, and imagine a short story in which these three ideas take place and in which the Querent plays the hero(-ine). As we use this three-card trick more often, we shall make a habit of embroidering imaginary stories into our narrative. We don't say that the story is the truth, but explain that the story is the sort of thing that would happen to a person of the same age (or a little older) and the same sex. It is not a thing you have to believe, but if you don't take too much care in thinking it out, you'll be surprised how often it is or will be true.

The diagram for a three-card trick looks like this:

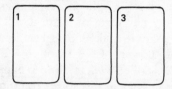

Position 1: An event that will happen – future event
Position 2: What the Querent will feel about it – future reaction
Position 3: What the Querent will do about it – future action
Because there are only three cards, it is difficult to use one card to amplify another. Yet, to a certain extent, the cards can be 'adjacent'. The cards describing the Querent's future event and future reaction will illuminate each other; they are to a certain extent adjacent. The cards describing future reaction and future action will definitely be adjacent. If the first card shows for instance the eight of Swords (criticism) and the second one shows the Chariot (emotion/passion), then if the third card were to show the three of Swords we would see, by its association with a fight or quarrel, that the Chariot's emotion would be anger. If, on the other hand, the third card were to be the Moon, it would show alienation, and we could guess that the Chariot's emotion was one of hopelessness or despair.

Because of its simple lay-out, this spread is often used at fairs or other commercial fortune-telling booths, where either a quick, or a superficial (or both) reading is required. It is easily remembered by beginners, becomes little used by more advanced readers, and finally comes into favour again when intuition has been fully developed. In a way, it is rather like that child's musical instrument, the recorder, which is played at school because it is fairly easy to make simple music with it (and is cheap to buy). Later, if the child is really interested, he will graduate to a proper silver concert flute; perhaps later in life the musician will discover the virtuosity and power of the recorder once more, but this time will really use the full powers of the instrument.

To make full use of this spread means developing one's intuition which usually comes after several years of constant use of the Tarot. However, very good results can be obtained when the Reader is drunk, say after a party (not too drunk, please), or, dare I say it, under the influence of other illegal substances; you might also try it when you are very tired, such as at the end of a long day or journey. These are all circumstances when you are tired or careless, and things flop out. I generally use this spread at the end of parties or after a long session of reading cards.

It is also a very good spread to use if you want to answer specific questions about circumscribed areas of interest, such as money or marital happiness. Just use one suit of cards from the Minor Arcana, or use only the Minor Arcana. This spread is not really suitable if you are using only Major Arcana cards.

* * *

The second linear spread is again a very traditional one used at fortune-telling booths by gipsies and by smart people in boutiques in Oxford Street in London. It uses 21 cards, which is why I'll call it the Pontoon spread. The cards are selected and laid, face-up, in groups of three, in a line of seven. The diagram below shows how:

Position 1: The character of the Querent
Position 2: Nearest and Dearest
Position 3: Fears and Hopes
Position 4: What is expected (and might not happen)
Position 5: What is not expected (and might happen)
Position 6: The Immediate Future
Position 7: The Distant Future

The way this spread is normally and traditionally used is for the

Reader to look at each little heap in turn and say something relevant about the subject. For instance, under the heading the Immediate Future it might have the six of Swords, the Knight of Cups and four of Rods, so the Reader will say that the Querent is going on a journey, will meet a dashing young man and probably marry him. End of chapter, and on to the next.

I usually start by looking at the 21 cards as a whole and simply counting the number of cards in the following categories:

1. The Major Arcana, of which there should be 6
2. Swords, of which there should be 4
3. Cups, of which there should be 4
4. Rods, of which there should be 4
5. Pentacles, of which there should be 4

Attentive readers will notice that the numbers add up to 22, when in fact there are only 21 cards. So sue me, I'm only giving round numbers, since I will not have the cards torn to satisfy sea-lawyers armed with pocket calculators.

A more discerning reader might ask where these numbers come from. Well, the total pack of the Tarot numbers 78, of which the Major Arcana accounts for 22. Those of you who know probability theory will understand, and the rest of you will need to simply accept, that if you choose a random 21 cards from 78, then you should expect 6 of them to be from the Major Arcana. Of the remaining 15 cards, you can expect there to be equal numbers from the four suits of the Minor Arcana.

Now in practice, the actual cards won't be anything like this in distribution terms. I asked my daughter of 11 to toss up a penny some weeks back in order to illustrate probability to her. The chart of throws looked like this:

The first twenty throws:	14 heads	6 tails
The next ten throws:	6 heads	4 tails
The next ten throws:	2 heads	8 tails
The last ten throws:	4 heads	6 tails
Total of fifty throws:	26 heads	24 tails

In fact, the more throws you make, the nearer the figure will get to evens. But in any given small number, the figures may be very out of balance. Mathematical probability looks at the *likelihood* of any card (or coin) coming up; it is now believed that in the long run the number of heads and tails would be equal. The mathematician is interested in the long run, although as the economist Keynes once remarked, in the long run we're all dead. The Tarotmancer is interested in the short run, and so we are more interested in the way the cards *deviate* from the probability.

If the spread of 21 cards contains more than 7, or fewer than 5, Major Arcana cards, the Querent is in some sort of trouble. Too many cards indicate either a lot of deep problems, or the *feeling* of deep problems overwhelming the person. Too few cards usually indicate someone who has problems, but won't look at them, or tries to hide them. The first type, with too many Major Arcana cards, will *tend* towards depression or even suicide if things are left too long; the second type, with too few, is typically someone who is cheerful in the face of troubles, helps out other people for many years, and suddenly runs amok at the age of forty. If you see more than 8, or fewer than 4, Major Arcana cards, try to talk with the Querent about their problems, explaining to them the reason why you feel that they do have problems to discuss.

If the spread has a large number of Major Arcana cards, have a look at *where* they are. A spread with nine Major Arcana cards, six of which are Character and Hopes and Fears, should lead you to feel you are dealing with someone with deep personality problems. If most of the cards are in Expectations and Not Expected, then perhaps the Querent has a too rigid attitude; too many cards in the Nearest and Dearest might indicate either that their friends are in trouble, or more likely, that the Querent tends to pick friends who are likely to get in trouble. Many people like 'rescuing' or 'helping' other people in order to boost their own self-regard – this applies to social workers to an alarming degree.

Some years ago I was asked by a mutual friend to give some advice and help to a young lady who was setting up a hostel for run-away teenagers who came to London thinking to make their fortunes. The young lady in question had no qualifications except boundless energy and enthusiasm; she had worked in a similar hostel for some years as a voluntary part-time worker, and realized the need for more hostels. The authorities gave her money to do up an old house which was scheduled to be taken down in three years but would do in the meantime, and also would pay for the salaries of the three qualified social workers needed to run the place. I gave advice on the design of the letterheads and the toilets, the heating and the kitchen; lastly I was asked to choose the colour-scheme. I thanked her, and said that as she was going to live in the place, she should choose, but could she please paint a large notice over the staircase:

THIS PLACE IS RUN FOR *OUR* BENEFIT, NOT YOURS
She got the point immediately, but the qualified social workers didn't like it one bit; one of them got very angry after it was explained. As the house was run on a democratic basis, the notice was never put up.

Having looked at the incidence of Major Arcana cards, we now look at the way the Minor Arcana is distributed. First of all, we count the Major Arcana cards, and take the number away from 21; the remainder is divided by 4. If there are eight Major Arcana cards, then take 8 from 21 to give 13, which if divided by 4 yields three sets of 3 and one of 4. Three Major Arcana cards should yield two sets of 4 and two sets of 5, and so on.

If one suit has far too few, and the other three sets about the same number, then we diagnose a situation where the Querent either is deficient in that particular attribute, or where they have tried to suppress or hide the attribute. Two Swords, and four each of Cups, Rods and Pentacles, might indicate either a stupid or non-intellectual person, or someone who has tried to hide their intelligence. Many people, such as teenage girls, try to hide their cleverness for various reasons. The teenage girls, for instance, often hide it so as not to frighten off prospective husbands. The trouble is, by the time they are married they are so adept at hiding that they cannot use it any more. Another frequently encountered suppression is that of artistic talent. Small children are either told they can't paint well enough (for the Art teacher, that is), or they are discouraged by the parent's attitude to art.

I have, on my desk, a permanent reminder of this. Some ten years ago I was asked to do some work for a school in South London. I had to meet the Headmistress about once a month for some six months; on the first occasion I noticed that her whole study was full of the work of her pupils, and I was particularly enchanted by a pottery elephant. It was crude, and didn't look very realistic or elegant, but was beautifully glazed and decorated. It was lovely, and I said so. The Headmistress immediately offered it to me, on condition that I would wait four months before collecting it.

The child who had made it turned out to be West Indian. Her parents could not understand the beauty of *naif* art; it reminded them too much of native African art, whereas they were striving to the glossy perfectionism of those Woolworth reproductions of little boys crying, or the full-bosomed Spanish beauty. The Headmistress assured me that the girl would not take the elephant home, since the parents would simply break it and throw the pieces away. The girl was leaving school in four months, and until then she had the legal and moral right to take possession of her artwork – she never did.

Back to our card-counting. If two suits have most of the cards, and the other two only a few between them, then this gives us a feeling as to the strengths and weaknesses of the Querent. The strengths and weaknesses will be the *combination* of the attributes of the suits involved (remember our 'emotional + angry' man of chapter 9?).

By now we should have a fairly interesting outline picture of the type of person our Querent is. The information forms a background to anything we see in the individual cards, and in a sense, the background has an 'adjacency' to all the other cards taken in turn.

You should now start looking at the individual positions. Each chapter has three cards, and each card has many possible, different meanings. Sounds rather like the man we met on our way to St. Ives:

> As I was going to St. Ives
> I met a man with seven wives.
> Each wife had seven cats;
> Each cat had seven kittens;
> Man, kittens, cats and wives,
> How many were going to St. Ives?

In our case, we have to learn to combine and choose. You can pick, using your intuition, *any* attribute of the top card in each pile; the second card is used to tell something else on the subject which might make us look at the first attribute in a different way, and this applies even more so to the third card. I think it is easier if I use an imaginary example:

The Querent has eight Major Arcana cards, three Rods, three Pentacles, two Cups and five Swords. I diagnose someone who has problems, is logical, reasonable, and perhaps an intellectual but has difficulty with his feelings and expressing emotions. If we now look at the chapter headed Hopes and Fears, we find the eight of Swords, the three of Cups and the World. I feel that the Querent is unsure of himself, and looks for criticism (eight of Swords) so as to become better; at the same time he is afraid of criticism because it will indicate disapproval. The three of Cups indicates that he likes to join groups or clubs in which he will find people who will criticize him, but that at the same time he only joins clubs where the criticism will be about his ideas, and not his feelings (remember he has too many swords). The World shows that he looks for approval from other people, or success in the eyes of the world. The combination of the three cards, plus the distribution of the twenty-one cards, tells me that I am dealing with someone who cleverly tries to join groups and make friends with people who are mainly interested in intellectual pursuits. These are places where his lack of emotional understanding can be successfully hidden from others, *and from himself*. This works extremely well until he meets someone who wants some sort of emotional tie, such as being his wife. And we can guess that the sort of deeper trouble he is in at the moment comes because his wife, girlfriend or friend is making emotional demands upon him, the sort of demands he has avoided until now.

In each group of three cards, we try to see what they have in common, or in what way one card gives greater insight into another. We can definitely say that each of the cards in any one chapter is adjacent to the others in that group. Again, try to tell an imaginary story about the sort of person to whom such a combination of attributes would apply, not bothering to try to make it true to the Querent but merely true to itself.

The example I gave just now, of the man with the emotional blockage, ended with the idea that one group of cards can make you suspect what is happening, and that you must look in another group to *confirm* your suspicions. That idea forms one of the most interesting and powerful methods of reading cards, and I think a little more discussion would be useful.

When we look at the cards under Character of our man, we see the Knight of Cups, the four of Swords and the Devil. The Knight loves them and leaves them, he's on the go and wants to get places and doesn't care about the consequences of his action; you might say the end justifies the means. The four of Swords indicates the search for rest after the battle is over; perhaps the Querent is rushing on so as to get the disagreeable messy business of life over and done with. Lastly the Devil indicates that the Querent is locked into all sorts of preconceptions and is unable to be free. I get here a picture of someone who is impatient with all the little illogical things in life, but just wants to earn for himself a quiet place where he can sit and think out intellectual problems which he feels are the *real* and important things of life.

If we couple our impressions of the man with regard to Hopes and Fears *and* Character, the composite picture emerges of a person who is impatient, energetic, intellectual, eager to win fame in some intellectual pursuit; his problems arise because he cannot see that the emotional side to Man is just as important, that cutting off emotions and feelings diminishes the person. Such a person is all right as long as they have no emotional ties with friends, family or wives and sweethearts.

So now I look at the Nearest and Dearest chapter. And sure enough, there it is. The Queen of Swords, the High Priestess and the Queen of Rods. Near him are one or more women who want to love him, give him support but who feel widowed. These may be his mother, his wife, his sister, his girlfriend; at different times they want to love this little boy who is so intelligent and loveable but cannot feel their love. It is in fact his inability to *feel* this love from people that has caused him to look for intellectual approval. But it will never give him the security that comes from *feeling* that people love him.

We see here the way that while one is examining one group one is stimulated into looking at another group. Generally speaking, in this lay-out, there are groups which are more often than not 'adjacent'. Character is adjacent to Hopes and Fears; Expected is adjacent to Not Expected. The combination of Character and Hopes and Fears with Expectations and Not Expected will help enormously in seeing what the immediate future has in store for him; the combination of Character, Nearest and Dearest and Hopes and Fears will tell us about his Distant Future. Perhaps the diagram below is easier to follow:

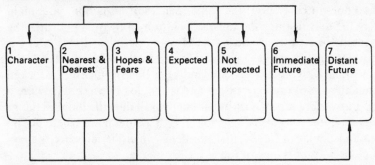

Each Querent will choose his or her own set of cards, and raise individual problems. The patterns of adjacency discussed above are only the *likely* ones to look for; there are many other possibles.

In linking 'adjacent' cards or chapters, you will often find that there seems no obvious connection. Try to think of all the different possible meanings of each card. For instance, in the chapter on Character we may find Justice, the Empress and the Queen of Swords. The three cards have in common that they all have a feminine figure on them, but in other ways they are quite different. For instance, the Empress is the card of fruitfulness, abundance and fertility, whereas the Queen of Swords has the idea of widowhood, barrenness, retentiveness. Justice carries the idea of responsibility, fairness and perhaps a little guilt; the Empress doesn't care very much *how* she gets what she wants, as long as she gets it. How do we combine the three ladies?

In a way, Justice is an abstract principle; we can say that Justice is above man. The Empress doesn't serve or support any man; men serve and support her. The Queen of Swords is a widow or a maiden aunt, without a man. We can now see that the essence of this character is the idea of independence from men – here is the 'cat that walks alone'. It applies whether the Querent is male or female. The connection between adjacent cards may be difficult to see, but it does force the Reader to associate freely and achieve insight.

* * *

The third linear spread I'm going to discuss is a purely intuitive one. After shuffling the full pack, the Querent is asked to choose a single card. This is turned face up and the Reader interprets the meaning or the attributes of the card as an event, just like in the three-card trick. The Querent then, and only then, picks a second card, which is turned face up to the right of the first. The Reader interprets this as a second *event* which will follow on the first. Every time a card has been interpreted, the next card is chosen, turned face up and put to the right of the previous. Series of between six and ten cards are all possible; there is no set limit.

From one point of view, this is one of the easiest spreads to lay and read. It is, however, totally dependent on the Reader's intuition. I find it best to try to get into the first stages of meditation before attempting this spread. Since you may either know nothing about it, or perhaps just as likely, you have a different system, I will describe what I mean by 'the first stages'.

Seat yourself comfortably, either upright in a chair, or on the floor, cross-legged with a small cushion under your bottom. Sit quietly for a few minutes and try to relax all your muscles. It helps if you tense them first, so that you can be aware of relaxing them. When you are quiet and reasonably relaxed, take a fairly deep breath, and release it slowly and steadily for a slow count of seven. Then breathe in again for seven counts, and continue breathing slowly and rhythmically for three or four minutes. You don't need to count after the first few breaths, but concentrate on making the breathing a smooth and even rhythm.

This is *not* meditation, but just an exercise leading up to it. After the breathing exercise, you are ready to try the spread. As each card comes up, handle it smoothly, and just say the first thing that comes in your head. Try to make the series of cards a continuing story about the Querent. It will generally help if you have used another spread, such as the Pontoon or the Celtic Cross (see next chapter), before using this one, so as to gain some general insight into the Querent.

I will give you an example of such a sequence. The cards will be the seven of Rods, the five of Cups, the King of Rods, the two of Rods, the eight of Swords and finally the Sun. If you have a pack ready, lay them out and refer to the cards before you as you read on.

The Querent will have to face a struggle if he wishes to develop his career (the Querent was especially interested in his career prospects) which he can overcome by standing up for himself. In the process he will achieve some happiness, but will regret the costs in terms of lost friendship and loss of personal innocence. He will meet and get to know a progressive businessman who will actively help him in his career. At this stage he will feel he has achieved almost all he wanted, but something is lacking; perhaps he feels that without help from the King of Rods he couldn't have made it on his own. His lack of self-confidence, and his dependence on the King of Rods, allow him to be exposed to and be sensitive to a lot of criticism; he feels helpless to defend himself. The last card, the Sun, is about personal happiness, so we can guess he learns to come to terms with himself and reject the criticism.

The spread described above has no 'adjacent' cards to the right or future side of the sequence. All the cards to the left or past are adjacent. Generally speaking, the series is ended when some card indicates 'the end' of the question in the sense that the marriage of the prince and the princess ends a fairy story. We sophisticated people know that a marriage is only the beginning of another story. Yet that doesn't stop our enjoyment of a fairy story. Similarly, here we must stop our tale of the young man's business prospects.

* * *

The three spreads are called linear because they are all laid out in a line, and because in reading them we start at the left and move to the right, in a sequence just as in a book. Certain cards and groups of cards are adjacent, but there is always a starting point to the sequence, a mid-story and an end. All linear sequences are at the same time very simple, and yet are the spreads needing and being able to absorb the greatest amount of intuition.

Finally, before I go on to the next chapter, with totally different spreads, I must tell you that there are many more linear spreads in existence. You can look them up in the many books on the Tarot; this book is not intended as a reference book. You will also find the same spreads shown above, but with the 'chapters' given different headings. Don't worry, there really isn't an authoritative, 'proper' way of laying out a spread. The important thing is not how you lay the cards, or what each card stands for, but how you link them.

Chapter 11

MULTI-LEVEL SPREADS

We now come to one of the most powerful patterns or spreads. This spread is used to analyse the psychological make-up of the Querent, his immediate, deep-seated problem, the alternative courses of action, and the memory of and attitude to the event he will have in the future. The pattern is called the Celtic Cross, and is shown in most books on the Tarot; each book will assign a different name or content to each station, but the pattern will look the same. There is no real demonstrable reason why the names and content assigned to the stations as shown in this book are the right ones, and you may prefer other ones. Remember, there is no one correct way, suitable for everyone. However, the pattern I am going to suggest shows definite advantages when we start connecting the cards.

In the diagram on page 118 Card 1 tells us about the immediate problem, the one which prompted the subject to come and have his cards read. The Querent may not always be aware of this on a conscious level, but will often recognize it when it is talked about during the reading. The second card 'covers' the first; this represents the course of action which will help the Querent to deal with the problem in a way that will help him to grow up. Card 3 'crosses' the first; this also shows a solution to the problem, but the solution is short-term, and leads to further problems, or the same problem in another setting and at another time. Card 4 shows the influence governing the subject's actions in the future, and Card 5 the influence in the past. Card 6 shows what actually did happen in the past to lead up to the crisis shown on Card 1 and Card 7 what will happen in the immediate future. In order to clarify, Cards 6 and 7 show *what* happened or will happen, and Cards 4 and 5 show *why*. Card 8

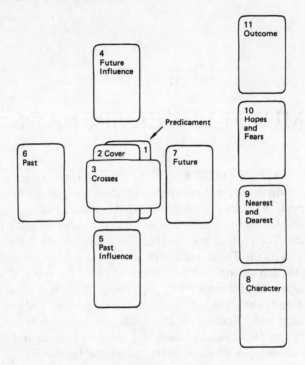

tells us about the most important character trait of the Querent with reference to the problem shown in Card 1. This character trait may not be the most important or recognizable character identification, but it is the one with the most bearing on the problem. Card 9 shows the Querent's nearest and dearest, card 10 his hopes and fears. Card 11 shows the attitude to and the memory of the crisis as seen by the Querent when the crisis is all over.

If you have followed events so far (go for an action replay if you need it), then you may well ask, why lay them in this pattern. Why not in a row, like the previous spread. The answer is presumably that the cards near each other have some kind of relationship; that the pattern itself shows some system of connection that enables us to read far more. I have discovered two possible patterns, and perhaps in the years to come I, or you, will discover further relationships.

The first pattern I have called the 'Flow of Events' and may be thought of as a broad arrow heading from past to future; in the diagram it moves from bottom left to top right. Students of the film, and especially of Westerns, will recognize that this diagonal division of the spread suggests movement. Looked at in another way, the arrow can dissolve gradually into an animal hide or even a pentagram, the symbol for human will.

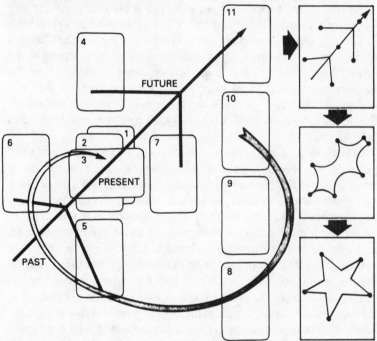

The Flow of Events shows how Cards 5 and 6 form the past, Card 1 the present with its various possibilities 2 and 3, while 4 and 7 form the future, leading eventually to the memory of it all at 11.

The second pattern I have called the 'Spiral of Influences'. It links up a number of cards to show why the subject is in the crisis now confronting them. Card 10, Hopes and Fears, may be likened to a carrot and a stick which drives Character, which in turn comes under the Past Influence to undergo the Past Event and so arrive at the Present Crisis. It must be emphasized that all the cards only reveal their content in relation to the Present Crisis; the Present Crisis can only be understood if we understand all the previous cards. So when we have followed the spiral we must go back to re-interpret all the previous cards in the light of the final one, and this process may repeat itself several times before a unity emerges. As the psychic mirror is focussed, more light shines on the area revealed, and it becomes easier to focus even more sharply.

At this stage, when we have gained a preliminary insight into what is going on, we may make use of one of the most powerful tools in opening the subconscious to the conscious. We ask the Querent to pick three cards from the spread before him, by pointing at the ones which most interest him, for whatever reason. Then the Reader must forge them into one concept to create synergetic energy. In chapter 6 we discussed synergy in terms of a definition; the definition would leave most of us looking rather blank, so let us take an example.

In the forest, a large tree has fallen over, and a great number of people are in need of firewood. The log is far too big to be moved by any one individual, so each person comes in turn, saws a piece of log just small enough to carry, and takes it home. Eventually, twenty people saw off and carry twenty pieces of the tree, and it is all gone; each person must saw a bit of the log before he can carry it home, and thus he will be tired through the sawing before he starts the carrying. Yet if all the twenty people came as a group, they could lift the log in one go, and carry it to a saw-mill, where it could be cut quickly and easily. A great saving of energy made only possible through the synergetic action of the twenty people acting as a group. Similarly, the new concept in the cards created through combining the cards will create a far greater insight which will be beyond the reach of any three single cards. In this particular spread, the three cards taken together will create a new meaning which is not specifically stated in any one card, nor is it a philosophical griffon (a griffon is a cross between a lion, an eagle and a dragon, with bits of each making up its body) with bits of the meaning of each card tacked together. It should create a new concept not in the regular procession of the cards; the new concept will be the most deep-reaching meaning to be read in the Querent's problem.

Let us take an example using the Celtic Cross spread. The Querent comes to us with a problem concerning his marriage; he suspects his wife is unfaithful, and what should he do? His spread looks as follows:

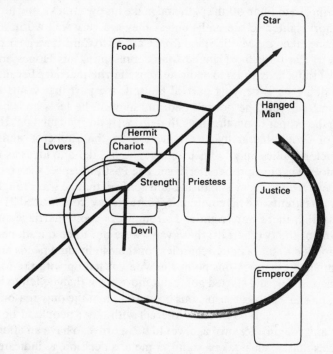

We will start with the Spiral. His Hopes and Fears are about dedication, i.e. he would like to dedicate himself to something but is afraid to commit himself, for reasons we don't know as yet. His Basic Character is that of the Emperor, and so he loves order, hierarchy, custom, precedence and rule by divine right (perhaps he has a touch of the Male Chauvinist Pig syndrome). Under the Past Influence of the Devil, which means here the preconceptions with which he was raised and which he did not see as such but felt them to be part of the way of all 'right-thinking people', he found himself confronted with the Lovers, i.e. a decision he had to take in his Immediate Past, which led him to his Present Problem, shown by the Hermit. His Present Problem involves looking closely at known paths to see where to go next; he has told us his problem is what to do about his wife's possible unfaithfulness. The Hermit wanders along the paths made by other men, peering with his lantern to help his short-sighted eyes see the well-worn path; but he is far too old and crippled to jump off the path and make his own tracks, and he is too short-sighted to see paths unless they are very well worn.

Having taken the Mystic Spiral from Card 10 to Card 1, we go back again to Card 10, the Hanged Man representing his Hopes and Fears. I think he is afraid to dedicate himself to his marriage because in so doing he is denying part of himself, the part that wants to remain free; yet if he doesn't dedicate himself, he feels he is not doing the proper thing, the thing that properly married men do. His love of order, hierarchy etc. indicated by the Emperor under Character applies only to his marriage; he has definite ideas as to who does what in a proper marriage. The Past Influence, shown by the Devil, would seem to indicate and confirm that he was brought up by his parents and his community (dare we say 'conditioned'?) to believe that there were right and wrong ways about marriage and the role of the two parties; these ways were not to be questioned, and applied to *all* people, regardless of their individual needs and potentials. Perhaps at this point the wife got fed up with the role assigned to her, and started going out more often than he felt to be right; he started to get suspicious because to him the only reason a wife would want to go out and interact with other people of both sexes and roughly her own age would be in order to have an affair. He feels that he must take a stand, come to a decision, as indicated by the Lovers; the only problem is what to do now? He is looking for a way to carry on the relationship amongst the known models of his childhood, and becoming more and more perplexed since these ways have changed since then. He has no real model to look to for ways to behave and cope with this crisis.

We now take a serious look at the Flow of Events. In the past the Querent combines the Devil and the Lovers; the idea they have in common is the idea of *pressure from outside*, forcing one to choose or conform. The Present Crisis, indicated by the Hermit, is the problem of not being able to make decisions outside his conditioning. The two alternative solutions to his problems are indicated by the Chariot, and Strength. The Chariot counsels allowing the emotions to take over, perhaps letting the heart rule for a change, instead of the need for propriety. This would let the Querent grow into a looser, less rigid and more loving person. If, instead, he heeds the card of Strength, and applies rigid control, then the pressure of resentment will continue to grow, and eventually it will reach such strength that no ordinary slanging match can contain the fury; there will be a physical fight, or perhaps a final breakdown of the relationship. The crisis the Querent is trying to solve now will be deferred to a later date by heeding the card that 'crosses'. The Immediate Future is shown by the Fool and the High Priestess; these have in common the idea of spiritual development. Under the Future Influence of starting a new path he will gain a connection with his anima, his conception of the ideal woman. He learns to listen to his guardian angel and the feminine, soft and understanding part in himself. Finally, in the long term, he will look back on this crisis as an event which taught him to learn trust, optimism and well-being.

However, we still haven't come to grips with the underlying problem and for this we now suggest the choice of three random cards to the Querent, taken from the spread in front of him. He chose the Fool, the High Priestess and the Lovers. What concept unites these three?

The Fool is associated with starting new paths, breaking out of his preconceptions and habits, of being innocent, and having luck. The High Priestess has to do with being mystic, supportive, connecting with the inner ideal of womanhood inside any person. The Lovers have to do with choice between alternatives, of making decisions, and starting new relationships because of that decision. I suddenly realize that all three participate in the idea of 'potential'; the Lovers have to do with the idea of choice between potential paths, or alternatively with the change from the potential of a choice yet to be made, to a kinetic energy kindled through the exercise of the choice. One of the choices of the Lovers is between the Bad and the Good. The High Priestess has to do with the potential of growing towards an ideal contained within us; finally the Fool is about the potential each one of us has of connecting with the Universal (God, if you like) that lies within us. Obviously, these are not the normal everyday meanings of these cards; they are special, rarely used aspects of these cards. They fit together to produce a new concept, the idea of 'Potential Ideal'.

If we now look at the whole problem, we suddenly realize that the real conflict in Hopes and Fears lies between the conformity to the ideals of marriage embodied in the concept of dedication on the one hand, and the need to realize the potential within himself which he believes is stopped by the need to fulfill his role as husband and father within that marriage, on the other hand. He is playing the game of 'If it weren't for them . . .'; if it were not for his wife and children then he could go off and become a famous writer. He can't at the moment, because he must support them financially, which he couldn't do if he were trying to be a writer. And the little slut isn't even grateful for his self-sacrifice. We suddenly see the Hermit in a different light, and realize that he is unhappy precisely because his rigid upbringing prevents him thinking of alternative ways out of his dilemma. The alternative choices of the Chariot and Strength now seem to mean the alternative between allowing his real feeling to emerge in such a way that he and his wife can discuss his ambitions and frustrations, and the temptation to suppress all these feelings as weak and childish. His future, the High Priestess, shows him beginning to connect his inner drives to his conditioned ideals, probably as a result of this reading.

Obviously, the advice the Reader can give is to see whether the Querent can change his preconceptions as to the proper role of the man and the woman in a marriage. At the same time, a full opening of the emotions, 'showing that he cares' may well have a good result, especially as we note from the Nearest and Dearest that his wife has strong feelings concerning her responsibility and guilt with regards to her own actions in the past.

The above attempts to show the inter-relationship between the eleven cards and the importance of pattern; the meaning of the cards in combination is more important than the meaning of the individual cards. Never be afraid to assign new, slightly unconventional meanings to the cards if you feel 'they are right' in any given spread, but use them only for that particular occasion.

At the very beginning of this chapter I briefly described some purposes for which this spread is particularly useful. I think it might be interesting to say a little more about it. For instance, I mention 'the psychological make-up', and this in itself might be all that we wish to gain from reading this spread.

If we have some idea of the character, the hopes and fears, the past influence and the nearest and dearest of the Querent, it should, if this information is pooled into a synergetic concept, enable us to understand what sort of a person we are dealing with. We can start with the two cards showing Hopes and Fears, and Character. These can definitely be said to be 'adjacent'; each throws light on the other.

The chapter in this spread headed Hopes and Fears is a very strange one to most people, in that they have difficulty in understanding that they can be represented by one card. The way out of this dichotomy is to realize that to most people they are the same. A good example is the expression 'God forbid' which any pious Jew makes after wishing his enemy bad luck, as in 'Moyshe, that bad-tempered old schnorrer, should break a leg, God forbid'. The pious Jew hopes for bad luck to Moyshe, but if it should come to pass that Moyshe really breaks a leg, then there will be a tremendous feeling of guilt.

Similarly, in our secret inner lives, we hope for all sorts of dreams to come true; yet conversely we are afraid that they might indeed come true. This can be due to the realization that such a hope is so impossible for us to realize that we don't even want to start; many people would like to be film stars, but few of us even try going for an audition as a film extra or for a drama school. It can also be due to the realization that it will mean sacrifices on our part which we are not prepared to make; many fat people dream of becoming thin but won't take the trouble of slimming because it means the sacrifice of eating which they need in compensation for other deep-seated troubles. Some of us are afraid to achieve our hope because then there would be nothing left to aim for, or to grumble about, or to blame things on, or . . . Try your own secret hope for size.

So perhaps you can now see how revealing the card on Hopes and Fears can be when read in conjunction with Character. If we now look at the Querent's immediate friends and loved ones, we can tell even more. As the old saw says, 'A man is known by the company he keeps'. The card will tell us what *sort* of relationships he has with people, or perhaps what sort of friends he likes to keep. Lastly, we look at his Past Influence to learn something of the Querent's environment; these are the influences that mould his character into a particular form. The gourd starts as a gourd, and grows up to be a gourd; but by confining it with string you can force it to grow in the shape of a bottle or a bowl.

The analysis of the Querent's psychological make-up cannot always be expressed in words, but its intuitive understanding by the Reader will allow for direct prediction of the Querent's reaction to future events or stimuli.

The second major use to which this spread can be put is to try to understand any deep-seated problems the Querent may have. The need for this arises for either one of two major causes. Firstly, the Querent may feel unable or unwilling to discuss any such problem. This could be caused by embarrassment, or by a desire to test the perceptiveness of the Reader. The second reason, the more frequent one, is that the Querent sees the problem at one level, and the Reader at another.

A good example of this might be as follows. A young lady comes to me and states that her problem is that she cannot find a man who really cares for her; she has plenty of attention, but it is of the wrong kind, and what she really is looking for is a loving, cherishing husband. I don't even pick up the cards, but merely chat with her whilst observing her. I notice she is wearing a very smart dress with all the right accessories; she has paid attention to all the fine points like hands, hair, nails as well as make-up and handbag. She has brought out her fine points, and has a habit of smiling at me as she talks, facing me but never looking directly at me with her eyes more than a fraction of a second. Her dress in no way conceals her physical charms, with which she is well-endowed; in every way she gives the impression of making every man she meets feel that he is attractive to her. Small wonder that she gets plenty of attention. She makes this habit of flirting a standard for every man she meets; she cannot know in the space of a few minutes what I, or any other male, am really like, and whether we would ultimately suit. Yet she acts as if she is attracted; this makes me feel that she is not looking for a husband, but just looking for some fun. The more she flirts, the more likely she is to attract fun-lovin' play-boy types, and the less likely a husband. Why does she do it?

Her Hopes and Fears are represented by Judgement; she wishes to get to know herself but is afraid. Her Character card is the Devil, which shows how much she feels locked in. Her Problem card is the Magician, who is somebody who uses his abilities for mundane purposes. Suddenly I realize that her real problem is that she is afraid that the type of man she really wishes for would not find her good enough; should she find him, he would disapprove of her. In order to avoid putting this to the test, she tries to attract a totally different sort of man, of whom *she* can disapprove. That way she avoids the danger of being judged and found wanton.

I can now say that her real problem is her lack of confidence in the goodness of her character. When she solves that problem, she won't need to flirt desperately with every man, and can instead spend her energy trying to attract the man who really matters to her.

Many people approach the Tarot Reader wishing to test his 'psychic' qualities. Their attitude is one of – 'If you can see the real problem, then I'll trust you'. This raises some very interesting points.

In the first place, is it important for you to raise their confidence? It is important to a commercial fortune-teller, who must earn enough to live on, and can only do so by inspiring confidence. That is one of the reasons why so many spreads incorporate details of the past or a description of the loved one; they are designed to demonstrate the insight of the Reader. After Sherlock Homes has demonstrated his acute powers of perception and logical reasoning, the reader is left in no doubt that all crimes can be solved by the great detective. The people seeking his aid certainly are, and it is only the stupid bumbling Watson who remains in doubt.

If you are claiming clairvoyant powers, then such a test is certainly a reasonable one. But if you see the Tarot as a means of gaining insight, of understanding and focussing problems and possibilities, then this test will not work, and will prevent the real power of Tarot intuition from working. For this reason, I usually explain that you can only get out of a reading what you put into it, and that anything I tell the Querent is designed to help the Querent, not the Reader.

Before leaving this interesting spread, I would like to mention that I feel this spread is best done using the Major Arcana cards alone. Obviously it can be done with the whole pack, or just the Minor Arcana, but I strongly feel that the type of questions raised and answered is best done using the section of the Tarot with the deepest meanings.

The other spread in this chapter on multi-level non-directional spreads is based on the Tree of Life. The Tree of Life is a diagram which is used to explain the relationship between Man and God and anything in between. It is the product of a Medieaval esoteric study of the Old Testament by Jewish philosophers but did not really become of great interest to Western occult students until Lévi and Crowley connected the Tarot with the Tree of Life. The study of the Qabalah is an interesting pursuit on its own, and there are plenty of books about it; all that interests us at this stage is the *pattern* of the Tree of Life:

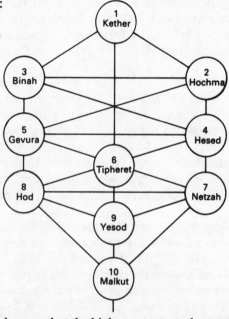

The general idea was that the higher you went, the nearer God, and the lower you went, the further away. 'Kether' means the Crown, and is the highest point Man can imagine, whereas 'Malkut' means the Kingdom (of things that you can hold and eat) and is identified with the body of Man, i.e. the body without the soul. There is a lot more to it, but for the present we are just going to take the pattern as a spread on which to lay out cards:

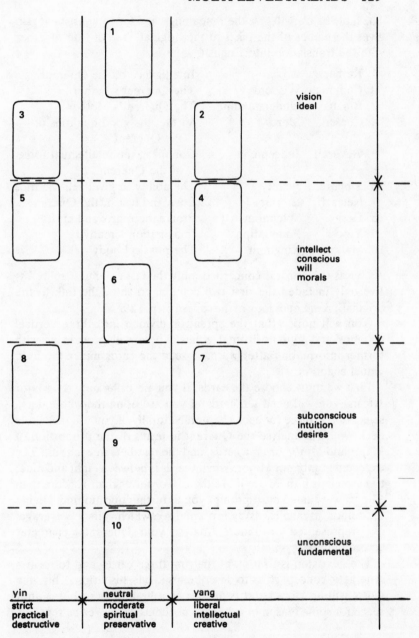

The table below will give their meanings, and for comparison it also gives the names of the parts of the original Tree of Life together with the translation into English.

1. Kether	Crown	Intelligence of the Querent
2. Chokmah	Wisdom	The Querent's Father
3. Binah	Understanding	The Querent's Mother
4. Chesed	Mercy	Virtue, the good qualities of the Querent
5. Gevurah	Judgement	Conquest, the intellectual force of the Querent
6. Tipheret	Beauty	The ability to give; self-sacrifice
7. Netzach	Eternity	Love and lust of the Querent
8. Hod	Splendour	Procreation, arts and crafts
9. Yesod	Foundation	Imagination, creativity
10. Malkut	Kingdom	The physical body

As far as the Tarot is concerned, only the last column is relevant; I've only included the first two columns to show the link to the original Tree. Let us look at the spread on p. 129.

You will notice that the spread is divided into three vertical columns and four horizontal zones. These will provide us with further information after we have read the cards under the individual chapters.

First we must choose the cards. If you are using only the Major Arcana you will need ten cards; if you are using the whole deck, select thirty, three for each chapter. Naturally, if you use the whole deck, you will analyse the Querent in terms of the proportion of Major and Minor Arcana cards, and the numbers in each suit. The expected number of Major Arcana cards is between eight and nine; be suspicious if there are more than 10 or fewer than 7. More than 11 or fewer than 6 must prompt you to further questioning. Divide the Minor Arcana cards by four, and see which suits are average, over-represented or under. Analyse your Querent's character accordingly.

The next step is to look at the first three cards, and to form a synergetic concept so as to describe his ideals, his vision. This, in a sense, will be Hopes and Fears; an area he aspires to but cannot reach for some reason or other. Some ideals will never be reached, and others will be reached after a new, higher goal has been formulated. Cards 4, 5 and 6 represent what the Querent thinks he can do, what he is able to do and feels he ought to do. Cards 7, 8 and 9 are about what the Querent would like to do, but feels he oughtn't – it's either illegal, immoral or fattening. The last card, from this point of view, represents the unconscious and instinctual parts of the Querent.

Now we look at the vertical columns. Cards 3, 5 and 8 taken together will allow us to look at the way the Querent is practical, strict, no-nonsense, and destructive; that the column is female should come as no surprise to those of us who have heard of Kali. Don't forget that things have to be destroyed before the new can be built; destruction is necessary. Cards 1, 6, 9 and 10 show the moderate, spiritual and preservative aspects of the Querent; these are areas of balance, of care and cherishing. The last column shows the aspect of the Querent that is male, creative, intellectual, liberal; the attributes we officially admire in Western civilization.

The three vertical columns give us a different way of looking at the individual than the horizontal way. It is almost as if we have first looked at his profile, and now we are looking en face. What we are trying to build eventually is a fully three-dimensional picture. Preferably in colour, with sound and movement. It is up to the Reader whether he combines the three or four cards in any column to give a single synergetic new concept, or whether he combines columns and zones in order to define the 'practical vision' (i.e. Card 3) of the Querent, as opposed to the 'creative desire' (i.e. Card 7). There's lots of scope to form adjacencies of concepts, rather than cards. Of course, if you have chosen to use the full Tarot pack, you can have a field-day.

At last we can get down to individual chapters, and talk about the Querent's father, mother, intelligence and so on. By this time you should know a great deal about the Querent, and the cards in each chapter should speak volumes.

As you have seen, we have descended in order from the spread as a whole, through taking parts of the pack, to individual cards. A full reading, using the Qabala spread of the Tree of Life, will take you at least an hour or so; in order to get the best out of it, use all the different levels.

Chapter 12

SPREADS OF DECISION AND CHOICE

Both the linear and the multi-level spreads try to find out and understand what the Querent is about. They cast some light on his make-up, his friends and loved ones, his problems, his past and his future. Historically speaking, these spreads have evolved from traditional fortune-telling, where the Querent was interested in what was going to happen. It is almost as if the people who believed in the Tarot also believed that your fate was written in the stars, or was in the cards, and that no struggle would avail. The classical Greek tragedies, such as Oedipus, show the prediction coming true precisely because the participants have struggled to change fate. I've always secretly wondered what would have happened if the father of Oedipus had not struggled; if one believes totally in predestination, then that is a silly question, since the father had no choice but to struggle. And yet . . .

Modern astrology is beginning to change its attitude. You will hear the phrase 'the stars incline, but do not command'. This parallels the twentieth century development of the science of psychology/psychiatry where it is held that early or innate character traits *tend* to make people behave in certain ways but that, with help, it is not impossible to rise above these compulsions.

I am inclined to feel that people will tend to do things which are predictable unless they struggle mightily to stop doing them. It is possible for a heavy smoker to stop smoking entirely, but requires tremendous effort; for a heavy smoker to become a light smoker is even more difficult. With smoking we are dealing with a habit which exhibits itself in such a way that it is easily seen; whenever you have a smoking cigarette in your hand, you know you are smoking. But how do you stop yourself from being rude to people? Or flirtatious?

When does being firm, in the one case, and friendly, in the other, become excessive?

I am of the opinion that there are two major ways in which people can change through the use of the Tarot. The first is the occasion when the Querent comes to the Reader at a 'node point'. The second is when the Reader is able to draw the Querent's attention to certain deep-seated problems which are not being tackled but are causing recurrent problems.

A node point is an occasion when the deep, underlying problems in the Querent's psyche cause a visible crisis. The Querent is aware of the crisis, and tries to solve that, even to the extent of consulting a Tarot Reader. If the Reader understands that the outward and visible crisis is a manifestation of an inward and invisible chronic problem, then it is possible to do something about the chronic problem by solving the acute crisis appropriately. We have seen something of this when we were discussing the Celtic Cross spread; the underlying, chronic problem was the Querent's inability to feel free to realize his potentiality, while the acute, visible problem was his need to know whether his wife was unfaithful. By suggesting a course of action that would change his way of tackling the visible crisis, it is possible that a change is made in the way of tackling future similar crises *and* of slowly changing his deeper psyche.

The second way of changing the Querent is by drawing his attention to these deep-seated problems *before* they result in a deep crisis. If, for instance, using the Pontoon spread, we notice only three Major Arcana cards, six each of Swords and Pentacles and only three each of Rods and Cups, then we can start thinking about the sort of problems this person is going to meet with in the future. At present the person is suppressing all doubts and fears, but seems lacking in feelings and has an inability to grow. As long as this person does not have a family or close friends, and everything practical in his life goes fine, there will be no problems. But family or friends will raise problems of a personal nature which will demand the use of his feelings to solve or at least deal with; practical problems cannot always be dealt with practically. By drawing the Querent's attention to the imbalance, it is possible to plant a seed in the mind which may grow to the point where the recipient will actually do something about it.

When the Querent comes to us with either a request for a general reading, or a request for an analysis of the general situation surrounding a problem, then we use a linear or multi-level spread. However, when the Querent comes to us for help in reaching a decision then we use one of the spreads which I will describe below. These spreads are for use when a decision has to be made whether to go on or stop, whether to act or not to act, and which of two alternatives to choose. They are designed to help the Querent *understand* his underlying problems; the Reader does not make the choice, but merely illuminates the underlying problems and leaves the final choice to the Querent.

As we are trying to find the deep-seated, underlying, chronic problems behind apparently acute crises, I would strongly recommend the use of the Major Arcana only. Remember, at this stage you are not trying to prove how accurate or 'psychic' you are; you are merely providing insight for the use of the Querent. If he doesn't 'believe' you because you have not provided any miraculous data about his past, that is his loss.

The first spread is one which I shall call the McCarthy spread – the man who said that those who are not with us are against us. We select seven cards and lay them out in the following spread:

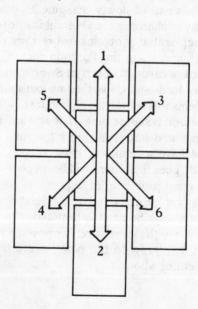

The cards are turned over and laid in the numerical order shown. Cards 1, 3 and 5 are designated as the positive aspects and Cards 2, 4 and 6 as the negative; Card 7 shows us the underlying problem.

Positive aspects can give reasons why the Querent should do whatever it is they are contemplating, or should persevere with whatever it is they are considering bringing to an end. Negative aspects suggest stopping things, not doing things. At this level of reading we are simply *telling* the Querent to do one thing or another.

In order to understand what is going on, we must firstly combine opposites. We take, for example, Cards 1 and 2 in order to see what they have in common. To do this, we must first understand an idea that was first mentioned briefly in chapter 8: the meanings of reversed cards. In traditional methods of reading, the reversed card has a different, often negative, meaning to the card standing the right way up. I suggested this was too simplistic a view, and that really any attribute is an idea which can range from one extreme to the other extreme.

Let us take the Major Arcana card Justice. It looks very like the lady on the top of the Old Bailey (the highest court in England), except that this one is not blindfolded. It is the absence of the blindfold that distinguishes the Tarot card Justice from the classical statue of Justice. Most people pay no attention to the absence of the blindfold, and feel that the card means something like justice, fairness, balance; at times they add things like responsibility or the consequences of previous actions. After reading the chapter on what I think all the Major Arcana cards mean, you may be no wiser or clearer as to what I feel the card means. But have a look at the following diagram:

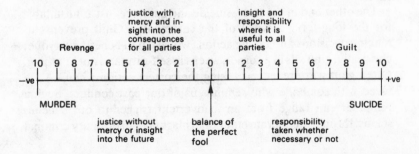

The card Justice covers the whole range from murder to suicide, neither of which will help the Querent solve the problem. In between are slightly more 'civilized' solutions such as revenge or guilt; gradually as the Querent achieves greater understanding of the real balance between extremes, he approaches nearer and nearer to the zero. Historically, civilizations have tried to move their official, approved solutions to problems from the extremes to the middle. We move from 'an eye for an eye' to the idea that a murderer is perhaps somebody who is merely sick; the Sumerian judges insisted that if you gouged someone's eye out, your own were to be judiciously removed, whereas we now would decide that an eye-gouger was perhaps mentally disturbed, and remove him for observation and treatment.

The reason Justice is not blindfolded in the Tarot is to emphasize the concept that ideally justice should be coupled with insight, the insight that realizes all the consequences of a decision. The need for the community to be protected from the actions of sick or wicked people must be balanced with the need to provide an opportunity for the accused to grow healthy enough so as not to feel the need to repeat the action – simply punishing him won't help. Letting him go completely scot-free won't help to allay the fears of the community. The needs of the present must be balanced against the needs of the future – light community service instead of a short prison sentence will turn a potential recidivist into a useful member of the community. Obviously, no earthly man or judge can know enough to make such a decision, hence we come to the realization that the card represents a range of values, a concept which can take all extremes and intermediate points and unite them into one card.

The other end of the scale, suicide and guilt, are just as unsuitable for the long-term survival of the community. Guilt prevents us making decisions and taking actions which could benefit everyone; classically, guilt sits in a corner, weeps in self-pity, and does nothing. Often guilt will prevent us taking the correct action when we are faced with someone who reminds us of our past conduct. Such a reminder can range from an inadvertent trigger to our subconscious, through deliberate emotional blackmail to ordinary criminal blackmail with menaces and threats.

Taking responsibility whenever it is possible, without seeing whether or not it is necessary or useful is nevertheless a good distance away from the still centre, but at least it is not as destructive. Its everyday consequences are either a feeling of guilt if the assumed responsibility proved too much, or an attempt to play Jewish Momma. Jewish Momma does everything, but *everything*, for her children while they are small, to the point where the children never learn to do things for themselves; when they are older and want to go out for the evening, Jewish Momma says, 'Go out, have a nice time, here's some money for a nice meal – I can afford it since I'll just have a sandwich tonight as I sit by myself in the kitchen waiting for you to come home. Don't worry, children, just make sure you have a nice time.'

Much nearer the centre lies the act in which responsibility is assumed when, and only when, it is really necessary. If there is an accident in the street, it is necessary to check that someone is redirecting the traffic, that someone is fetching medical help, and that first-aid is being given. Satisfied that these things are being done, we can move on, instead of standing in the way giving orders and volunteering for all sorts of duties which can be done better by others.

Back to our spread. You can now see in what way we should combine opposite cards such as 1 and 2, 3 and 4, and 5 and 6. Each of the combinations should form a synergetic new concept for which these two cards are extremes at opposite ends of the scale.

Card 7, at the centre, represents the *real* problem, and each of the pairs of cards at opposite ends of the arrows, must be combined in turn with the centre card, to form a triad whose synergetic new concept is being sought. As this is beginning to sound very complicated, with lots of big words being thrown in, I think an actual example might be useful.

A young lady comes to me asking whether she will go on holiday to Spain with her boyfriend. After a little questioning it comes out that the actual location is not important, Italy being just as good; it is clear that it is the relationship with the boyfriend which is in doubt.

She selects seven cards, as follows:

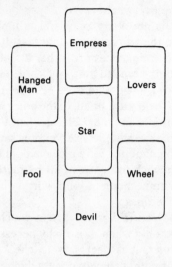

I straightaway look at the Star, and I feel that the real question has to do with trust, i.e. the extent to which she trusts the young man. Will he look after her, not only when the going is easy, but when she is in trouble, ill, pregnant, bad-tempered and so on? She looks to the holiday as a way to get to know these things about him, but to a certain extent realizes that the holiday itself will require that she trust him. Should she really go on holiday with the young man?

We'll assume that the Hanged Man, the Empress and the Lovers are cards which suggest that she should and will; the Fool, the Devil and the Wheel suggest caution and alternative holiday arrangements. Let's first take a look at the combination of Hanged Man and the Wheel. The Hanged Man is about dedication, spiking your flag to the mast, whereas the Wheel is not attached to anything, is free to go when and where, and drifts with the current. Now add the central card, the Star, and see what unifying concept is created.

Here it seems to me that this is a line about putting all your possessions and talents into a partnership, trusting that such an investment will be returned. If she goes on holiday, she will have invested all as a sign that she trusts the young man with her all (question; is she a virgin?). If she doesn't go, then she is free from a tied investment, and can make another choice; the sad thing is that she won't be going anywhere, but will just drift. If she goes, at least she will be going somewhere, even if it is only to Hell in a handbasket. So we can ask her legitimately whether she prefers to commit sins of omission or commission.

The second pair that catches my eye is the Lovers and the Fool. The Lovers is about decision, while the Fool is about innocence and starting new things. Add the Star to this combination, and search for the unifying concept to find the idea of security. You see, at one end the Lovers gives the security of having made a decision, and the comfort of not having to worry about making decisions in the future; at the other end the Fool is just about to start something of which he doesn't know the ending. If she goes to Spain, she has committed herself and she doesn't have to worry about any future decisions. If she doesn't go, she will probably lose this boyfriend, and have to look for a new one; she isn't sure whether she can find one. The Fool's innocence also suggests strongly that she is still a virgin, and perhaps a strong desire for sexual experience lies behind the idea of going to Spain.

Lastly, the Empress and the Devil need to be looked at. Combined with the Star, the trio suggests the need to find out her powers and ability to be an adult. The Empress is a fertility symbol, a woman who can have children and be a mother. The Devil is the symbol of being locked in; frigidity is one way of looking at it. Perhaps she feels that going to Spain will prove that she can *be* an adult through doing what is normal for adults, i.e., making love. If she stays away, she cannot trust in herself and her maturity.

Summing up all these conflicting ideas, we can say that if she does go to Spain with her boyfriend, she will feel a sense of commitment, she will be able to prove that she is an adult rather than a little girl, and she will not have to worry about making a decision or having to look for another man. If she stays at home, or goes elsewhere on her own, she will be free to explore other men, she can put off committing herself irrevocably, and she can still enjoy part of her childhood.

Finally, I look back at the Star, and realize that it can also stand for the idea that each individual is at the same time part of the whole Human Race, or of the Cosmos if you like. All of us make this decision at some time or another; as the human race has survived, by and large, these decisions must have been the right ones on most occasions.

After we had looked at all the cards, and discussed the meanings, the young lady realized that the reason she wanted advice was because she wasn't ready for marriage yet, and she felt that the trip to Spain more or less meant some form of commitment. I suggested a short love affair with a man who wasn't interested in marriage might help a lot in sorting out her real feelings. But I would not predict the outcome, nor make any commands. I felt she was old enough and sensible enough to make up her own mind.

* * *

The second spread which is best suited to making decisions I will call the three-decker. You can use either only the Major Arcana and pick one card for each position shown (seven in all) or you can use the whole pack, and pick fifteen. Let's first of all look at the diagram of the spread:

If you use the combined pack, lay down the first three cards in position 1, then the next three in position 2, and so on to position 5, which needs only one card, as will positions 6 and 7. If you are using only the Major Arcana, lay the first seven cards in the positions as shown.

Chapter 1 tells us about the problem; chapters 2, 3 and 4 give us various different solutions; chapters 5, 6 and 7 tell us something about the consequence of the various solutions, 5 being the consequence of solution 2 and so on.

Let us look at the chapters in greater detail. Starting with Card 1 it will by now be obvious, if you have read the earlier sections of this book, that this is designed to give us the underlying problem of which the query presented by the Querent is only a manifestation. Now, whereas the previous spread was designed to look at alternatives, this spread is not designed to make choices but to examine whether there is a way out of what seems a static, locked-in situation.

Generally speaking, people behave as if there are at least two, and sometimes more, ways of getting out of a nasty situation, or making a choice. This is because they look at the manifestation of the underlying problem; they want to solve the immediate problem and move on to a pleasanter time in their lives. This still leaves the chronic problem, and sooner or later it will manifest itself again; that is the reason why we can predict in the Tarot. But if the Querent can be persuaded to do something about the underlying problem then the recurrent crises won't recur.

Looking at the underlying problem demands that the Querent listens without filtering ideas through the preconception that there are two or more alternative solutions, one of which is the better choice. For the underlying problem, there is one way of getting out of it, and a number of ways which leave one locked inside the dragon.

But if there is only one problem, and one way out of the problem, that doesn't mean that there is only one thing that the Querent must do in order to escape. There are several aspects of the Querent's psyche which will all need to be worked on; these are depicted by Cards 2, 3 and 4.

In each human being there is an area which revolves around ideas first taught by the parents, and later reinforced by the morals and ethos of the community in which the Querent grew up. Some psychologists/psychiatrists call this area the Super-ego; others call it the Parent. This is the area where people talk about what they 'ought' to do, talk about 'duty', talk about 'they'; they mention 'conscience' and 'God' and such. This is the area where people do things which they don't want to do, but feel they must because otherwise they would feel disapproval; the disapproval from their parents, their friends, the community, or God. This area is shown by Card 2.

Card 3 shows us the area which corresponds to the rational, logical area of the human being. In the school of psychology/psychiatry called Transactional Analysis this is called the Adult; classically this is called the Ego. This is the area of reason, of things being done after all the alternatives have been weighed, of decisions made on the basis of facts. It is the least interesting of the areas of a human, but the most important from the point of view of survival.

Lastly, Card 4 governs the area known classically as the Id, and the Child in Transactional Analysis. This is the area of desires, of wants, of things we would like to do; dreams, wishes and ideas.

All three areas are necessary for the members of the human race. The Id/Child gives us the ideas and dreams that provide us with both the wish and the energy to live; the Super-ego/Parent stops us carrying out ideas which are harmful to the community (and thus ultimately to ourselves); the Ego/Adult mediates between the two and carries out the resultant. The problem shown by Card 1 needs to be dealt with at all levels; we may find that the Super-ego/Parent needs to be less severe, the Adult/Ego less logical and rational, while the Id/Child needs to be listened to and strengthened.

To sum up briefly what I have said so far, Card 2 shows what the Querent feels he 'ought' to do, Card 3 what he feels is the logical thing to do, and Card 4 what he would 'love' to do.

Now we can discuss Cards 5 6 and 7. These represent the consequences if the Querent only attacks the problem at one level. If he only changes his Super-ego/Parent then the type of thing shown by Card 5 will happen, and so on. If, however he tackles all three levels as suggested by Cards 2, 3 and 4, then the result will be to reach a new level represented by the synergetic compound of Cards 5, 6 and 7. I think all this can be most easily seen if I set it out as a diagram on the next page.

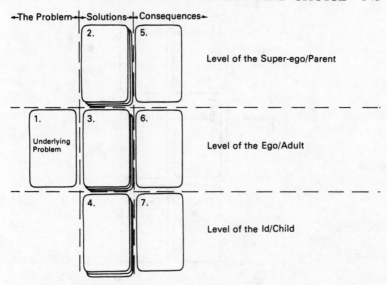

Let me show you an actual example, taken from my files (as they used to say on some of the minor horror films that followed the main event).

The Querent is a lady who is married, about twenty-five years old, no particular material problems, has a one-year-old child, and a happy marriage. She feels lonely and has difficulty making friends; they have recently moved to a new part of the country. It is far from her family and friends; she asks me if she will meet new friends. After some talk we agree that it isn't quite so simple, and we try to find out what is really going on.

She picks seven cards from the Major Arcana, and the spread is shown on page 144.

The Moon represents the underlying problem, and I felt this was really about alienation, the feeling of being alone in the world with all other people too far off and too uninterested to love and feel for the Querent. Such a feeling of other people not being interested often prevents the alienated person from responding to any overtures of interest and friendliness which are offered.

I lived for many years in a great metropolis, a city that was known for the many lonely people who live in it. I never experienced that

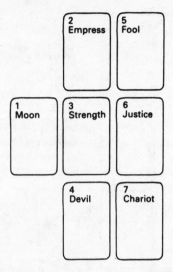

loneliness, but a glance at window advertisements, newspapers and just the faces of people showed the feeling of loneliness that soured the lives of many people. One day I went with a companion into a wine bar, and we sat at the corner of a long table at the back of the room. Our backs were to the actual bar and to the entrance, so we couldn't see people as they came in. After a while a gentleman came in, and took a seat at the corner diagonally opposite us, so as to face the direction of the door. In front of him he placed the weekly news-sheet of an organisation that was set up to allow lonely people to get together and be miserable in each other's company.

After a while, a second person wandered in, noticed the paper, and with a glad cry asked if this was the meeting. The two started talking cheerfully. Gradually the whole table filled up with further members of the group, which is so large that few members know each other by sight or by name. Every newcomer sat next to the previous arrival, starting with the gentleman in the far corner. Eventually the table, large as it was, became fully occupied; the last two arrived and sat next to my companion and myself. These last two were obviously unsure whether I and my companion were part of the ensemble. We smiled encouragingly, continued drinking our wine while the four or five people immediately adjacent started a conversation. Our immediate neighbours were half-turned towards the rest of the group, till, as the conversation turned to the pleasures of Amsterdam, I made a contribution (I have lived there) to the conversation. Immediately our neighbours turned back from their awkward posture and said, 'Excuse us, we didn't realize you were part of the group.' I replied we weren't and was astonished to see our neighbours turn back to face the main group, almost as if we weren't there. Ignoring our existence the conversation continued and shortly after the group went out on their appointed round of activities.

I realized at that point that the reason these people were so lonely that they had to join a club designed to lessen loneliness was that overtures of interest and friendship were not taken up joyously, but were examined and pondered. People make their own loneliness.

Back to our Querent, otherwise she'll get impatient. Card 2 (the Empress) shows that her Super-ego/Parent was strongly influenced by her mother, and that it had many preconceptions about the nature of things. Mother always said that men who pretend to be friendly are only after one thing. Mother said that women who immediately try to be chatty are not to be trusted. Mother said that one's family comes first, and that if you let too many people in, one of them at least will try, and be able to, harm you. Mother said . . .

Card 3 (Strength) shows how the Ego/Adult copes with this strong Mother's instructions. She keeps her feelings of loneliness under control, and keeps herself to herself; men who are friendly, women who are too chatty, and people who want to be too intimate are all carefully excluded by her being firm and rejecting such advances.

Card 4 (the Devil) shows what the Id/Child feels. Locked in, all the fun's outside and elsewhere. There's also a strong attraction for the physical side of friendship, the companionable embrace of other women, the flirtatious touch of another man. The Id/Child very much wants out, but can't because of the strong Super-ego/Parent and Ego/Adult.

If the Super-ego/Parent is dealt with, i.e. the lady tries to stop listening all the time to what her Mother said, then the result will be Card 5, the Fool. She will be without support, starting a new path without knowing where it is going. She will be without a guide or a set of comforting laws on what is right or wrong. She will flounder, and never feel that comfort of knowing that somewhere, somebody approves of her.

If only the Ego/Adult (Card 6) is dealt with, then she will act under the attributes of Justice; she will try to overcome her conditioning and make friends, but she will realize that her inability in the past was really due to her own attitude. This will bring on feelings of guilt caused by her sense of inadequacy; as she tries harder to make friends, each failure or set-back will make her feel more inadequate and make future overtures from other people seem even more suspicious.

Lastly, if only the Id/Child (Card 7, the Chariot) is considered, then the likelihood is that she will become swayed greatly by emotions, passions, great loves and great hates. Escaping the moderating influences of the Super-ego/Parent, and the sensible ideas of the Ego/Adult, she will indulge in unnecessary clandestine love-affairs, have love/hate relationships with bosom friends.

If, however, she does something about all her levels; if she stops doing always what Mother says, stops trying to find out what people mean when they say hello and gives in to her impulses to be friendly with the 'wrong' people, then the combined trio of the Fool, Justice and the Chariot will yield the concept of Courage. The Fool has the courage to set off on a new path with unknown destination; Justice has the courage of her convictions; the Chariot has the courage to fight and to express emotions.

Courage is what the lady chiefly needs. The courage to defy her Mother, to accept other people's overtures, and to give in to her own feelings. I wish her the best of luck and a joyful life.

So we see that this spread is about choice, but not the choice of whether to join a club specialising in lonely people, or not; the choice is whether to do something about your deep-seated problem, or let it go on passively. The donkey says to the horse, 'I never kick the same stone twice,' and the horse replies, 'But you don't miss a single one'. This spread is designed to teach you to pick up your feet so as not to kick *every* stone on the path.

Chapter 13

DESIGNING NEW SPREADS

If you diligently visit the library and borrow books on the Tarot, if you rush into every occult shop and examine what stock they have, and if you dip into the books belonging to your friends, you will eventually gather many dozens of different spreads. In the little notebooks I keep on me to record such finds I have in the order of fifty spreads.

Many of these use the same pattern of laying out the cards, but give the chapters different names. Others use the same names but lay them out in a different pattern. I have shown you the chief types in the last three chapters; I think you will find all traditional spreads to be variations on these basic types.

So, with all these spreads available, why do we need to design new spreads? Couldn't we find an existing one somewhere to suit our needs? Well, the answer is rather like shopping for bread. If you go into the average, medium-sized super-market, you will find perhaps five different brands of sliced, white bread, two brands of sliced, brown and an unsliced, white French loaf. The baker round the corner has more loaves of unsliced bread in various shapes and sizes, as well as sliced white. So far you have a choice between about twenty different loaves; but none of them are wholemeal brown bread. Aha! you can go to a little shop down the road which sells health-food and really healthy bread. When you've bought the bread, and tried it out, you will find out that they make their bread without enough salt.

I like bread made with wholemeal flour and plenty of salt. So I make it myself, despite the fact that I can buy anything like thirty or forty different types of bread within the town I live in. That is how it is with Tarot spreads. Most situations only need a standard spread, just like most people only need white, sliced bread. A few people need a little used spread, just as only a few people insist on wholemeal bread. And just on the odd occasion you will need to make your own bread, or spread.

A second reason for designing new spreads is the change in attitudes to Tarot and to the human psyche. We change our attitude, and instead of using the Tarot as a fortune-telling device, we begin to discover new uses to which we can put the system. And as we change from considering the fate of the Querent as fixed and immutable to considering it merely very difficult but not impossible to change, we need to use new spreads.

The first type of new spread was designed in response to a need to discover something about the health of the Querent. It arose out of a weekend class I conducted some years ago; the class was held in London and drew a mixed crowd, interested in many other things beside Tarot, such as astrology, alternative medicine, alternative types of psychotherapy and numerology. I decided to give an exercise to the class, namely to ask them to design a new spread as a group exercise. The eventual result used some of the specialized interests of all the members of the group.

We first of all decided the need for knowing something about the Querent's past medical history, a diagnosis of present difficulties and a prognosis of the future development. Just like in conventional medicine, it corresponds in the traditional Tarot to the Past, the Present and the Future. The numerologist considered three a good number.

We now discussed matters, and eventually we decided to divide the body into six different areas, as follows:

1. The psyche
2. The nervous system, including the five senses
3. The mechanical system, specifically bones and muscles
4. Lungs and heart
5. The food-processing system, including liver, kidneys
6. The reproductive system

By laying cards for each different area, it should be possible to build up a picture of the Querent's health. The numerologist felt it needed a seventh card, and the alternative medicine fanatic felt that the person as a whole had to be considered. So we added a seventh card:

7. The health of the Querent as a whole.

Each of these areas, seven in all, was to be considered in the Past, the Present and the Future. This seemed to satisfy all the members; Teacher gave them a pat on the back, and has used the spread ever since, with very good results. The official pattern of the spread is shown on p. 150.

Obviously, we use the whole 78 card Tarot deck, and we analyse the way Major Arcana, Rods, Cups, Swords and Pentacles are distributed (Major Arcana should be 6) in order to give us some idea of the Querent's character.

At this point, I must confess that the second spread in the previous chapter was another 'designed' spread, which came into being after I started becoming interested in Transactional Analysis. I use it for amateur psychotherapy, and it seems to work. It is a good example of a spread designed in response to changing attitudes towards the human psyche.

I would like to finish this section of the book by discussing the subject matter of spreads. The Querent comes to us with a question, or several questions, to which he seeks an answer; often I try to redirect the question to a more fundamental problem in the Querent's psyche. But every now and then, a question comes up which cannot easily be dealt with. The temptation is then to design a new spread to answer the question. Before doing so, it is well to consider some types of question for which the Tarot is *not* suitable.

The first one is time. The Tarot mainly analyses people as different types, and produces answers in terms of: 'When this happens to the Querent, he will react with that.' Other possible answers are: 'This is the sort of thing that is likely to happen to the Querent, because that is the sort of man he is.' But the timing of the stimuli, or events, in the life of the Querent is not subject to the Querent's character, other than that, 'This type of event is something that is more likely to happen when you're turning forty.'

There are spreads specifically designed to tell us when something is supposed to happen. We can lay out twelve cards in the shape of a circle, designate the first one as January and so on, to tell an event that will befall in each month of the coming year. This is mere

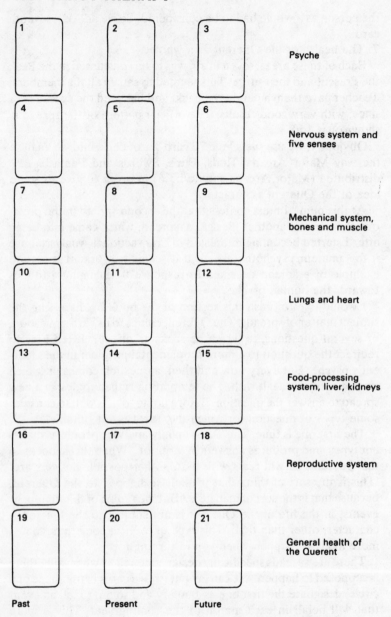

1	2	3	Psyche
4	5	6	Nervous system and five senses
7	8	9	Mechanical system, bones and muscle
10	11	12	Lungs and heart
13	14	15	Food-processing system, liver, kidneys
16	17	18	Reproductive system
19	20	21	General health of the Querent
Past	Present	Future	

fortune-telling, and there is no particular reason why it should come true.

I feel very strongly that the art of astrology is far more useful in predicting when the crises will occur, when the good sides of the Querent's nature will be uppermost. The use of bio-rhythm is another method of predicting node-points, critical times and periods when either the good or the bad parts of one's psyche will prevail. With the coming use of the computer, it should be possible in the not too distant future to programme a computer to chart crises points for several years ahead. At present it takes about half-an-hour to work out, using tables, a chart for a single point in time (usually at the point of birth); the idea of a continuous chart showing all future conjunctions, oppositions etc. would require a small computer. Such small computers are almost on the market, and I look forward to combining the Tarot predictions of *what* will happen with the astrological chart of *when* it will happen.

The other major area inaccessible to the Tarot is the analysis of the Reader by him or herself. In my classes I use an analogy and say that it is not possible to see objectively one's face. We use the mirror every day, sometimes many times, so we all think we know what we look like. Yet very few people can look at a photograph of themselves and instantly agree that it is a good likeness. To drive the point home, I then take a photograph of a person in the class, taken *en face*. The photograph is then enlarged to plate size ($6\frac{1}{2}'' \times 8\frac{1}{2}''$ or 16.5×21.5 cm). At the same time I turn the negative over in the enlarger and print a reverse copy, also plate sized. I then cut both photographs very carefully in half, down the centre of the face. I then take the left half of the photograph that is printed properly with the right half of the reverse printed copy, and stick them down on some card to produce a face; similarly the right half of the proper photograph with the left half of the reverse print. The end result is two faces which are completely symmetrical, but which don't look as if they are of the same person.

An artist will notice that every feature on a person's head is skew. One eye or ear is bigger than the other, and sits slightly higher. The slant of the mouth is hardly ever horizontal. It is usually possible to tell identical twins apart by looking at their faces, and drawing an imaginary line through their eyes and an imaginary line through their mouth. If these lines are made longer and longer, eventually they meet, either to the left or to the right. One twin will have lines meeting to the left, the other to the right.

But very few people can see their own malformations, unless they are very gross. Similarly, people cannot see their own psyche, because when they are watching themselves to see what sort of psyche they have, all they will see is an unnatural 'posed' idea based on the latent preconceptions they have of themselves.

It is possible to read the cards on the relationship between the Reader and another person, because we are looking at the relationship, or at the other person.

Other than the subjects of time, and of self, I see no restrictions on the subject matter of the Tarot spread. I will go into the type of questions most often asked, and how best to phrase them, in a later chapter called Archetypal Questions.

part four

Chapter 14

COMMUNICATION

Part 2 was devoted to individual words; part 3 was about putting those words together to make sentences. Perhaps you imagine that is all there is to it, and that, with a bit of practice you will now be able to read cards for all and sundry. Gentle reader, I must disillusion you; there are still parts 4 and 5 to deal with before I have passed on all the information necessary to reading the Tarot. Part 4 is devoted to the idea of communicating the ideas that the Reader has to the understanding of the Querent. Chapter 14 is about telling the Querent what you have seen in terms he understands. Chapter 15 is about speaking the same language, and chapter 16 is about translating vague general questions into precisely formulated questions which can be answered by the Tarot.

Let us start with the problems of communications. Communication includes the use of words as well as the use of silence. We meet this everyday when we ask someone, perhaps a small child, whether they have knocked over the Wedgewood vase while we were out of the room. If the child says 'No' then we are no wiser; if the child says 'Yes' then we know at least that the child admits to it (but we don't know if the child is covering up for a friend or a young brother). But if the child says nothing, and hangs its head to avoid meeting our eyes, then we know that it is guilty, and also feels guilty. The absence of words is a very strong form of communication in this case.

The very use of words can stop communication. A friend of mine, who is a psychiatrist in a very mixed area, tells me that when working-class mums come in with a problem, they will have difficulty in talking about their problems. They will talk vaguely of back-aches or the frequencies of headaches; only when you actually get them talking about their troubles you can really start helping. Some people have the opposite problem: they tend to talk so much that they miss the opportunity to listen.

Many people feel vaguely unhappy, without quite knowing why. Other people feel unhappy, and will tell you at great lengths exactly why, and how it is the fault of such and such, about which nothing can be done. If you have such people frequently around the house, and listen to their problems, then over a number of years you discover that most of their problems stem from an inability to communicate. They may talk too much, or too little, but they are not really telling you anything.

What does communication mean? We can think of examples of methods of communication, such as talking, writing, painting, music, T.V.; there is nowadays an enormous 'communications industry'. An industry implies, in this modern commercialized world, that there is a product or service that requires work to produce, and for which money has to be paid. The money is paid because some group or other finds it worthwhile to try to contact another group, and tell them something or other. They cannot communicate without the paid help of some part of the communication industry. In what follows I will be thinking in particular of the part that advertising plays in financing this communications industry.

Imagine a large company making chairs. The company has a factory with a lot of machines, a large number of skilled workers, and a number of decision-making managers, accountants, secretaries; in fact they have everything that is needed in order to make a large quantity of chairs. You must also imagine a large number of people out there in television-land who want chairs. Perhaps a few of them will pass by the factory and see the chairs inside; they can go in and buy one if they see the foreman. But that only sells a few; outside in the wide world are thousands of chairless people looking for chairs, while here is a factory which can satisfy that want. But neither side knows exactly where the other is; they are not communicating.

The company makes an historic decision – it decides to advertise. First of all, they have to announce they exist. If they were simply to put up posters saying 'We make chairs' and nothing else, that wouldn't help anybody. People would ask themselves who these chairmakers were, so the company must decide on an *identity* for itself, a name of some sort or another. Potential customers can then ask a shopkeeper for a particular brand of chair. 'Aha!' says the shopkeeper, 'you will be wanting the Tarot chair.' We nod, that is just the chair we've been thinking of, only we couldn't remember the name.

The company decides to call itself the Tarot Chair Co. By identifying itself, it allows people to distinguish *this* company from all other 'makers of chairs'. However, by identifying itself, it has given people some hint of the sort of company it is. They have elected to be known by a symbol, in this case 'Tarot', which will allow customers to guess a little or even a lot. Customers might guess that the manufacturers are interested in the Tarot; they might well be people who are interested in 'alternative' living (whatever that might be) and because of these attributes of the symbol we might guess that they are a little less 'business-like' than other companies. So the first rule is that identity creates image. In fact, of course, most commercial companies try deliberately to create image, as much image as possible, and as good an image as possible. Very blatant 'image-creating' names, like for instance 'The Cumfi-Chair Co.' might make us suspicious; we might decide that any company trying *that* hard might not be very honest.

Similarly, the individual coming to ask a question, will identify him or herself. They will say, 'my name is Mr Brown', or 'my name is Joseph Brown' or 'my name is Joe'. Other people will say, 'call me Dick', or 'most people call me John, but my real name is Jaranowskogaszy'. A person can be baptized James Pollard Robertson, but he may be known variously as Mr Robertson, Robertson, James, Jim, Jimmy, Pollard, Polly, Poll, J.P. or whatever; perhaps he is usually called by a nickname such as Racky. His choice of name will tell you a lot about himself.

Back to our chair company. Having given themselves a name, they must then decide where their address is. Their factory is somewhere in the country, amongst other dark satanic mills. Do they announce their address as being at the factory, or do they rent a smart office in London. If in London, is it to be in Belgravia, or

Bethnal Green? Belgravia is perhaps ten or twenty times as expensive, but then you can sell chairs for perhaps twice as much as you would get for them if your Head Office was in Bethnal Green. Again, with the individual coming for a reading, do they talk about themselves as being born in a private nursing-home, educated at a fee-paying school (English public school), living in a town-house, and working in the City? Or does he explain that there was no hospital in the neighbourhood where his parents lived, that the private school was one for children with learning difficulties sent there at public expense, that he lives in a flat over a chemist shop, and that he works as a messenger? The Head Office of the Tarot Chair Co. can be a tiny room in Belgravia or a huge building in Bethnal Green; there is no way of telling if you just phone or write letters.

Our chair company now announces its intention to supply chairs to the public. Well yes, it makes chairs; so what? Other people make chairs, what's so special about these chairs? Tarot Chair Co. chairs are comfortable, they look nice, they last and they are cheap. That's what they all say, is there nothing specially exciting about Tarot chairs? And here we come to the difficulty the company has in telling people what is so special about its chair. The fact is, the company doesn't know itself; it has simply never thought about it.

Most people with a problem will tell you at great length about their 'problem', especially if they are articulate and are used to verbalizing. Just like some companies which spend incredible amounts of money simply to tell you that their chairs are bigger, better, more comfortable, cheaper, etc. than any other company's products. But that is not communicating, that's just shouting. Not until companies, or people, learn that merely shouting is not communicating, can they even start learning what communicating is about. Not until the little boy stops howling that he's hurt can we start learning how and why he is hurt. People, and companies, when told they're merely shouting (or crying, or moaning, or bitching), will immediately protest. You might even believe them, if you didn't perceive that *all* the companies are shouting. Believe me, and you will if you have a look at the posters for beer, cigarettes or cars. It is sometimes very difficult to find the facts about these products. In the same way, we might believe that people are telling us about their problems; usually they're not, they are merely letting off steam. The only fact they are communicating is the feeling they have that they are in trouble. The only fact the advertisers of beer, cigarettes or cars communicate is that they are eager to make a profit, and that's hardly something we need to be told. Mere shouting will communicate something, but rarely will it be the something that really needs to come across.

A good example, well known amongst sociologists and sometimes, but not often enough, to managerial staff, is the Hawthorne experiment. This was the name of an experiment undertaken in the 1930s to see what effect lighting levels (the amount of light reaching the objects on the worker's bench) would have on productivity. It was commissioned by a company selling lighting equipment, who obviously wanted to prove that the more light was used, the higher the final productivity reached. So they got together a group of ten or so workers and set aside a special room in which they could work. The room had also special equipment to lower and raise lighting levels, and also other equipment to measure the worker's output. Specialist observers and scientists watched everything; the workers were chosen, and the experiment was explained to them.

At first, when the lighting level was increased, the output went up. Increase the levels by 10%, output went up by 6%. Increase the lighting levels by 20%, output goes up by 10%. Increase the lighting level by 30%, and output goes up by 13%. Obviously, at some point, increases in the lighting level will not increase output any further. At some stage in the experiment, they lowered the lighting levels to below what they were for the rest of the factory. Lo and behold, the output continued to rise. The light-bulb manufacturers threw up their hands in despair, but the sociologists now really got interested. After some years of thinking and repeated experiments, it became apparent that the increase in output was mainly caused by the way the workers had been treated. They had been given a special room, learned middle-class professors had talked to them as if they were human, attention was paid to their surroundings; for the first time in their working lives they were being handled as adult human beings, and not as slightly recalcitrant, biological production units.

Similarly, when workers in a factory go on strike, it may well be that they talk about more money, comfort, clean w.c.s or even, God help us, about the swear words used by the foreman. Their real problem is that they feel unloved, looked down upon, ignored by managers who do not see them as people. They cannot or do not want to communicate this feeling, and so they shout by going on strike. The individual needing help, or the company with a product to sell, needs to find out what it really wants to tell us.

The Tarot is a system which can help in rewording the problem in such a way that either the problem can be discussed, or even that the answer can be seen at a glance. In the real world of the chair company, very often an outsider can wander round the factory, have a look at the chairs made and how they are made and by whom, and come up with a flash of insight as to what it is that makes the company so special – the thing that makes a product into a Unique Selling Proposition, something that no other chair has. The chairs made by the Tarot Chair Co. are the only ones made by spiritually enlightened and pure people, the only ones that are made with an insight into the needs of the user from a psychic point of view. They are also comfortable, cheap, hardwearing and beautiful, just like all the other competitors' products, but only theirs are made by the Tarot process. Whether that actually helps to sell the chairs is another matter, but at least they have communicated an item of real information to the general public.

What they have communicated is another matter. The chair company may be very sure of what they mean by the phrases 'spiritually pure' and 'enlightened interest'; they really think they know what they are saying. The problems surrounding the actual meaning of symbols were discussed earlier in chapter 7, and they apply here.

Having identified themselves, given themselves a background, found their Unique Selling Proposition, and explained it in terms which most people will understand sufficiently well, the next problem is to reach those people of interest to the company; in this case potential chair-buyers. Chairs are used by everyone, but only bought by certain people. It is no good advertising in children's comics; it is no good advertising expensive chairs in papers bought by the masses. So we must identify our likely audience and talk to members in terms they are able to understand. When we read the cards, we gain a great deal of understanding with regard to any given person; if we want to tell these people of some of our findings, we must tell them in a way they can understand. We must also tell them things they are interested in.

A young girl who recently moved to a large city and is working as a shop assistant will understand if you talk about being poor and being lonely. Will she understand what it is like to be rich and lonely? To her, rich people can afford to have a house big enough to entertain, with enough money to buy food and drinks, a car to go off at weekends to see friends. How can such a person be lonely? Will she understand what it is like to have people around you all the time who pay attention to you because they want to obtain some or all of your money, people who are interested in being helped through the rich person's influence, or who merely like the creature comforts supplied by a rich person? So, if you want to talk about a type of loneliness, find a person who is interested in such matters. One aim in working with the Tarot is to try to understand, to feel, all conditions, in order that people with any sort of problem can come to us and be sure of being understood. Simultaneously, we must make sure that what we are trying to tell them is said in such a way, using their symbols and language, that they are sure to understand.

So when someone comes to us with a problem, we first of all try to talk a little with them. Make them a cup of tea, and ask about them, their ideas, their likes and dislikes. Then gradually lead up to the point where they state their question. Usually, they will talk about all sorts of things that upset them, many small problems they have; you must try to get them to come down to one, and only one, really important question. It may be very necessary to guide their conversation towards being specific, and here we run the danger of bullying people into stating a question just for the sake of it. Go carefully, and when they have come out with the real question, lay the first spread. Very often this first spread will merely give you further information on the problem that particular person has, the one they didn't even know existed. Go on discussing that problem, and lay a second spread to probe deeper. Again, don't merely announce the results, try to discuss. I generally try to tell the Querent what the chapter headings are, what are the particular meanings of the cards in the spread, and how the meanings change as we find 'adjacent' cards. Each reading, if there is time, is used as a platform for a miniature lesson in the Tarot. Ideally, after ten or fifteen readings, the Querent should be capable of using the Tarot him or herself.

When both Querent and Reader speak the same language, real communication becomes possible. In the meanwhile, it is up to the Reader to talk to the Querent in a way that the recipient understands. To help you, and to make you face some of the problems encountered, I suggest you play a game which can be fun if entered in the right spirit. I call it:

ARCHAEOLOGIST

If you are playing this by yourself, have a look in your pockets, your handbag, wallet, or the desk you work on. Set aside an object such as a coin, a label, a packet of matches, or some other object which is very commonplace. If several people are playing, it is more fun if only one person chooses the objects.

Now imagine you are an archaeologist living a thousand years from now. Perhaps there has been an atomic war, or Earth has been overrun by Martians; in any event, this object has been found as they were digging the foundations for the new rocket factory, and nobody knows anything very much about it. So there it is, in front of you, and you have to find out what it is, where it came from, what it is made of, what it is used for; by inference you must also try to discover all about the civilization in which this product was used. You must imagine that you have many machines and computers which can analyse the precise materials, and perhaps even translate the language.

Write down all the facts about the object, and the people who made it, that you can think of. If you are playing this game in a group, you can then challenge opinions, and the premises upon which you base your reasoning. Try to use your fantasy to think of logical yet totally different functions which might be attributed to such an object if seen by someone living a thousand years from now.

LETTERS

Try writing a letter to the head of Personnel of a large company explaining what use can be made of Tarot cards in staff selection and relations. You must explain things using words and phrases he understands and will accept.

Try also writing a letter explaining why European people find it necessary to save up in order to buy a house which has been built by a builder, including the concept of interest; this letter will be addressed to an African tribesman who counts his wealth in cattle, and barters for the rest, and whose housing consists of wattle-and-daub round huts with a thatch roof. Remember, his house costs virtually nothing, but he will have to pay for his wife, often using cattle, and more cattle than he can afford at the time.

Lastly, if you have strong left-wing political feelings, try your hand at writing a convincing pamphlet on behalf of a right-wing party, but without giving up any of your ideals. You must try to restate your ideas in a different language. Obviously, if you tend to vote right-wing, you write a left-wing pamphlet. If you have no strong feelings, then write both, and let that be a lesson for you to come off the fence!

Chapter 15

TRANSLATION

The previous chapter was about communication, the use of words, gestures, names, silences to convey information from one person to another. There are always difficulties in communicating because people are not trained to communicate. They may lack contact with their own feelings or with the feelings of other people; they may not have the vocabulary to express their ideas; they may lack the experience needed to feel easy when talking about what is going on deep inside them. Near the end of the chapter I referred to an idea concerning the need to talk to people in a language they can understand. This chapter is about the use of such language.

By training I am an architect, and for many years I trotted around designing buildings, and getting them built. Most people, and that includes architects, think that architecture is about making some nice drawings on some arty paper, and then handing over the design for technicians and builders to make into reality. My experience has been that the actual design with the soft pencil on arty paper takes perhaps 10% of the total time; the rest is spent first of all working out the cost of the design, and making sure it comes within the tight limits set by a money-conscious client. Then I have to convince Local Authorities that the building will conform to their legal requirements. Next the engineer has to translate my pretty design and work out how strong the concrete or the steel needs to be. After that a builder has to look at the result and give me a price for the building. Lastly the men who do the actual physical work must understand what has been drawn and written, so as to put the brick or timber in the right place. Each person, whether he be accountant, government official, lawyer, engineer, builder or labourer (and there are many others) has to understand what needs to be done.

Each talks in a different language, and each will need to have different drawings and instructions from me.

Sometimes, it may happen that a builder will deliberately choose to misunderstand me, so that he can make greater profits. Mostly misunderstandings occur because the architect and the builder talk different languages. The architect is very often a person with a middle-class background, brought up in a home with lots of books, where things are done with paper; if you want to have a barbecue in the back-yard, then you order one from a catalogue and write it off as an entertainment expense on your tax form (for overseas visitors). The builder will often grow up in a home with no or few books, but if the family decides on a barbecue, then Dad will knock one up himself, or perhaps get one of his mates to do so in return for papering his living-room.

A funny illustration of this difference is to watch an architect talk. He may be talking about something totally outside his own speciality, such as the class-system; suddenly, he will ask for paper and pencil, which he will use for making a vague series of squares and circles to 'illustrate' what he is talking about. In actual fact, his argument is no clearer, but he feels happier having paper and pencil to hand. The builder, on the other hand, will be able to listen and remember everything said, but if he has to say something, he will prefer to show you the problem using real bits of wood or pipes or whatever.

On the actual building site, these differences of language can become very noticeable. While still training, I was asked to supervise the pouring of some concrete. The concrete arrives in big lorries and is then moved by chute and wheel-barrow to the timber mould; it is poured into the mould where it will set, after which the mould is taken away, to leave the clear grey concrete form we all know and love. In order to make sure that the concrete gets to all parts, and that includes going in between some very complicated metal reinforcement bars, it is moved about using what is officially called a 'vibrating poker'; it looks like a long flexible vacuum-cleaner hose with a three-foot solid 2" diameter cylinder at the end. I will leave it entirely to your imagination as to what such a poker is called on site. The poker is thrust into the concrete and as it vibrates, the concrete pours much more easily into all the nooks and crannies; its proper use will make the concrete stronger. But if it is used too much, then all the cement in the concrete will pour out and settle near the bottom, and the big stones will stay on the top – this is bad concrete. So the poker is not used too much or too long.

One of the men on site was using the poker too much and too long. He was cautioned repeatedly, and asked to refrain from too long a usage; being a simple farmer's son, this had little effect. Eventually I approached him, pointed at the poker, and told him to use it the way a *young* horse uses it — in, out, and ready for the next mare. We had no more trouble. It was merely a question of using images and a language which he could understand. It helped that I had learned to speak some of his language; I am not fluent, but I learned enough.

Many of these language difficulties arise because we think that as we are speaking the same language, such as English, or French, we will understand the words used by the speaker. It is easy to assume that communication between architect and labourer is easy as long as the architect doesn't use long words. The real problems are much greater than merely using simple words. In order to gain some understanding of these difficulties, let us have a look at the idea of a foreign language.

This book will have been written in English, and is intended for an English-speaking or reading public. It may well be so successful (who knows?) that eventually it will be translated into other languages. The translator is someone who knows both languages very well; he will read the book in English, and then try to say exactly the same thing in the second language. It can be a mechanical, not especially well-paid, exercise.

Another person, who also knows both languages, will be critical of the accuracy of the translation. He will object that the subtle nuance of a word hasn't come across, or that the translator has used one meaning of the word and translated it into the second language, rather than another meaning. For instance, the English word 'cleaving' can mean splitting something, such as a block of wood; it can also mean joining together, such as when we speak of husband and wife cleaving together until death do them part. Many words have much more subtly differentiated meanings, or are more easily influenced by the words around them.

If you know both languages very well, you can compare the two, and criticize the translation. If you don't then it is still possible to compare different translations of the same work, done by different people. It may be that one translation tries for accuracy, while another tries to give a very readable translation.

There are occasions when I find myself listening to a discussion about philosophy which is being held in English, because the people who are participating can all speak and understand English. They may be French, Dutch, German, English and American; they will try to communicate in English. One person who is admired for his penetrating insight and marvellous ideas is by origin Dutch; he speaks in English, and sometimes his sentences do not make sense. This is often caused by his use of complicated English words which are an exact translation of *one* meaning of a Dutch word into *one* meaning of an English word. It all becomes much clearer to me when I translate his ideas into Dutch, something I can do easily, since I too am Dutch. I will then translate my understanding of what I think he meant into English, and often this clarifies his meaning for the rest of the group. The same happens with every speaker whose language is not originally English.

Such a double translation becomes very interesting, and is done far more often than is realized. The notorious play *Salome* by Oscar Wilde was originally written in French, and translated by Wilde's good friend Lord Alfred Douglas into English – or so Wilde would have us believe. But at the trial in 1918 of *Rex* v. *Billings*, Lord Alfred testified:

> 'I translated it into English. Of course it was a farce really, because Wilde really wrote the play in English, translated it into French, and got a French author to correct his numerous blunders and mistakes; he then asked me to translate it into English; and then when I finished my translation he revised it and put it back into its original language.'

More recently, a computer was programmed to translate from English into Russian, a useful piece of work since so many scientific ideas would then be available quickly. A second computer was designed to translate from Russian into English. To test for accuracy, the phrase 'out of sight, out of mind' was translated into

Russian by one computer, and the Russian version into English by the second. Out came 'if blind, then mad'. We laugh at first, but then perhaps we start to realize that the computers had made a very accurate translation, by selecting only part of the meaning and choosing the wrong part.

We can therefore check the accuracy of a translation by having the translation rendered back into the original by a second translation. If we give instructions to a child, or a soldier, or to a labourer we can check the accuracy of the transmission of information by asking them to repeat what we have said, *using their own words*. Similarly, most of us have had the experience of trying to explain something complicated, something that we have recently learned. Only as we tell it to someone else do we suddenly realize that we hadn't properly understood it at the time, and that we do understand it now as we explain it.

In order to make the whole issue a little clearer, I often ask my students to play a game which I call Translation. You can read the rules, read the examples and 'play the game' by reading this book; but you will not gain the insight that comes from actually playing it. So try to find two or three other people, perhaps as many as ten, and sit down with paper and pencil.

TRANSLATION

One person will think up a sentence, or perhaps a very small poem such as a haiku, and write it down. That person will then strike out words such as *of, and, in, a,* and so on. The words that are left are written down, and perhaps look like a newspaper headline, something that takes a few seconds to understand completely, but in which the most important words catch our eye. The person will then write down, next to each remaining word, another word which has a similar meaning. This last group of words is then read out aloud to the rest of the group.

The rest of the group take down each word as the 'first translator' reads it out, and make their own translation by thinking of a similar word. Eventually, when all the words have been read out and translated a second time, each member of the group tries to put the re-translated words together in one sentence, adding in any words such as *and, is, the, of,* etc. The sentences are read out, one by one, and compared with the original.

Here follows an actual example:

I composed a short sentence, a basic cry for help often heard in this badly organized world:

'I'm <u>starving</u>, please <u>give</u> me <u>food</u>, my <u>parents</u> have <u>left</u> <u>me</u> <u>alone</u> in the <u>world</u>.'

The underlined words are the important ones, and all the other ones were left out, so as to give:

'Starving – give – food – parents – left – me – alone – world.'

Underneath the key words I wrote down words which I felt to be roughly equivalent, as follows, and in the same order:

'Empty – transfer – necessity – providers – gone – speaker – solitude – environment.'

This last group of words, starting with 'Empty' and ending with 'Environment', were read out to the group of seven students.

Each student listened to the list I read out, and then put his own translations next to each word, and finally put his own translations into a sentence. Below are the results; first comes the list of re-translated words, then the re-translated sentences:

For 'Empty': Shallow, Half-full, Hollow, Gone
For 'Transfer': Project, Gone across, Pass on, Change, Seek
For 'Necessity': Need, Suffering, Mother of, Close, Important
For 'Provide': Give, Supply, Take care of, Paths
For 'Gone': Lost, Not there, Left empty, Forsaken, Went, Disappeared
For 'Speaker': Subject, Talker, Talk, Mouthpiece, M.P.
For 'Solitude': Loneliness, Alone, Isolated, Lonely
For 'Environment': Surroundings, Place, Dwelling, Seed of Life, Locality, Area.

'Not-lived-through suffering comes back to the one who just speaks, not acts, as loneliness and same surroundings.'

'There is a need in man to talk, when others are not there the world seems to have passed on and alone can be a hollow word.'

'Now that my mouthpiece has forsaken me, and left me hollow in my lonely dwelling place, to whom shall I turn to care for me . . . Ah, the mother of invention.'

'The P.A. system deafened the surrounding countryside: "Lonely, foresaken, in need of someone to take care of you? Fear not, simply have 'Empty' tattoed on your forehead." '

'She went, I felt isolated, others close talk with me, I now move on alone to seek the seed of life in other paths ahead.'

'The M.P. spoke of providing important total renovations to these lonely forgotten areas.'

Well, as you can see, some of these re-translations captured some of my original simple request; others were seeing my problem through strange spectacles. See if you can do better.

A second game I would like to suggest is not really a game at all. It is a custom which has become part of reality for many people. The game was introduced to me under the name of 'Buzz-words'. There are two ways of playing this game.

The first way is to draw up three lists of long, complicated words, and especially 'in' words whose meaning nobody quite knows. Such a set of words might look like this:

1.	2.	3.
penetrative	synchronous	framework
energy	systems	analysis
bionic	parameter	locus
feedback	positive	set
disparate	analogue	condition
in-house	sociometric	lattice
etc.		

By using a pin, or dice, or whatever, you pick one word from each list, and put them together to form a phrase such as 'disparate systems condition' or 'penetrative parameter analysis'; if possible, go the whole hog and form a sentence using such a phrase. Now look up, in a good dictionary, what the words really mean, and then try to find an example of the thing, using a common object or idea. The first phrase can be translated as 'a state in which 2 or more systems cannot be compared because they are too different', and then translated once again as 'comparing chalk with cheese'. The second phrase translates ultimately as 'seeing how far you can push your luck'. Have a go, it's great fun.

The second way is to think of a word or phrase, and then translate it into an alternative version. An example from George Orwell reads:

> Objective consideration of contemporary phenomena compels the conclusion that success or failure in competitive activities exhibits no tendency to be commensurate with innate capacity, but that a considerable element of the unpredictable must invariably be taken into account.

The original, from Ecclesiastes 9:11 reads:

> Again I saw under the sun the race is not to the swift, nor the battle to the strong, nor bread to the wise, nor riches to the intelligent, nor favor to the men of skill; but time and chance happen to them all.

In fact this was a game we played at college while studying architecture; it was officially approved on the grounds that by 'restructuring our visualization', we might be freed from preconceptions! Calling a staircase a 'vertical access corridor' or a low point in the garden wall between two houses a 'neighbourhood inter-action point' is fun; the end wall on a terraced row of houses becomes an 'open-ended, closed-lattice end condition'. The ultimate in this sort of logorrhoea is the circumlocution adopted if you want to avoid saying simply 'Yes'; you can, instead, 'create an affirmative response situation'. So there!

If you play these various games, and try to understand how they reflect the reality, then you will at least realize how much translation is required when you are reading the Tarot, and listening to the Querent's problem, and trying to suggest possible solutions. Being aware that between each person and every other person is an invisible gulf caused through a lack of common language will draw your attention to the need to listen and speak with understanding.

Chapter 16

ARCHETYPAL QUESTIONS

People say they want help, when they want attention. They say they want to listen when they want to be heard. We know this by what you say, by how you look, by what we can feel. Everyone else would feel it too, if they were not similarly self-absorbed and uninterested in you. You must first of all find out from yourself if you want to learn, and why you want to learn. If you go somewhere to buy something you must first earn the money, and have some idea of what you need. If you just have idle wants, and do not know your needs, you have a long way to go. If you become diverted from us by your behaviour you would never have been able to keep pace with us, anyway.

If this sounds unpleasant, it does not signify that it is meant to be unpleasant. If you think we are unpleasant, you are holding up a mirror to yourself and saying 'Look at them!'

(Salahudin Afranji)

That rather long quote from a Middle Eastern philosopher, written in the Middle Ages, is to my way of thinking apposite to the whole study of the Tarot. Its major point is the careful differentiation between want and need.

In the social science of Economics, a careful distinction is made between desire and demand. Desire is the (presumed) wish of the citizen to obtain some service or object. That means nothing; I can desire a private aeroplane or a Taj Mahal in my back garden, but nobody is going to lift a finger to supply these items. Demand is defined as the desire *plus* the willingness and ability to pay for it. If I have a million pounds in my bank, then I can find someone who will supply an aeroplane or a copy of the Taj Mahal.

In the study of the development of the psyche, a careful distinction is made between wants and needs. Wants are the things and ideas that the person desires; needs are the things and ideas that are necessary to his development.

Here I am, talking about developing the psyche, when all you wanted was to know how to read someone's fortune. Well, in reading a person's fortune, you are predicting what will happen given the Querent's present disposition and intentions. In order to change the future, it is necessary to change the Querent's psyche, and in order to understand the psyche we use the Tarot (or psycho-analysis, or tea-leaves or whatever). If you read someone's future, and leave it at that, it's rather like looking at a neglected garden and saying how messy it is and leaving it at that. A messy, neglected garden can gradually be cleared so as to become beautiful; an overgrown psyche with too many weeds, thorns and nettles can be weeded and cleared. The prediction that a garden, which is at present neglected, will in two years time be a jungle is only half the story. The statement that if five minutes a day is spent on weeding then in two years time the garden will at least be tidy is the other half; whether the owner will listen is another matter.

Let us take this analogy much further. The Querent comes to the Reader, and complains that his garden is not producing much fruit, and that the fruit is small, unappetizing and often diseased. Will next year's crop be better? A fortune-teller will look at the garden, and say that next year's crop will be worse, or better; someone interested in gardens will look at the garden, and try to understand *why* the crop is not good enough. He will sample the soil, inspect rainfall records, ask what fertilizers have been used, whether the garden is watered, and how and at what time of the day; he will ask how old the fruit-trees are, and what strain. Eventually the reader will find out that the man has used no fertilizer, or the wrong type, that the strain of fruit-tree is wrong for the soil, that the last three years have had far too little rainfall, that the owner has been pruning them in the wrong way for many years, or hasn't pruned them at all.

The Reader then puts all the facts together, and comes to a conclusion. It could be that circumstances have changed (rainfall, new insect-pests) and that the owner has not realized these changes, and has therefore not responded. It could be that the owner has been doing the wrong things, through ignorance or obstinacy. It could be that the owner has been lazy, or absent; he hasn't given the garden the attention and care it needs. Having reached those conclusions, the Reader then can say that, given the owner's willingness and ability to change the way he treats the garden, there will be an improvement or no improvement.

What the Querent wanted was to be told whether next year was going to be better. What he needed was to be told why it was not good enough, and how that could be changed. Things don't happen by chance, they happen because we arrange our lives so as to make these occurrences likely. Obviously, I'm not talking of train crashes or earthquakes, but of failed jobs, broken marriages, betrayal by friends, lost opportunities, depression, etc.

Of course, when we have told the Querent what needs doing in the garden, that doesn't mean that things will change. The Querent may object that too much work is needed, the fertilizer costs too much, the instructions are too complicated, that perhaps next year the old amounts of rain will fall down. That's O.K., you're not going to be able to do the work for him. But you can advise what needs doing, and that is the purpose of reading the Tarot.

Each Querent will come to the Reader with a different question. Some want to grow bigger roses, others want to reach roses which smell nicer. One man wants to grow giant marrows, another likes to sit in the garden and enjoy a book – is all that weeding really necessary? The questions vary enormously, and we have to deal with them, and discern the real need behind each question. Once the *real* question has been carefully exposed, we can get down to looking for an answer. How do we get at the real question?

For a start, it is in order to look at the Querent, and ask him, 'If, as you sit there, a man suddenly appeared right in front of your very eyes, whom you knew, without a shadow of a doubt, could answer any question completely and accurately; suppose, that you were allowed only one question, what would you ask?' Most Querents look a bit startled, and say something like 'I don't know, I never thought about it like that'. If a Querent can state that question, then spread the cards and get on with it. For the others, I have devised a formula, or rather a series of formulae, into which all questions can be translated, that is, all really important questions. Below is the formula, followed in each case by the type of spread that is most useful:

HOW/WHAT: Use a multiple-level spread like the Celtic Cross or the Tree of Life
METHOD: Strike out the words that do not apply.

How What	will shall ought	I he she we they	(ever) (not)	succeed be happy be sad resolve stop get on do think believe	(at all) (in)	my his her our their	marriage job relationships studies work life etc

SHOULD/OUGHT: Use a spread based on decision or choice, like the McCarthy spread or the three-decker

	should ought	I he she we they		succeed in be sad be happy do believe stop resolve	(about)	my his her our their	marriage job relationships studies work life etc

WILL/EVER: Use a linear spread such as the three card-trick, the Pontoon

	Will	I he she we they	(ever)	succeed in be sad be happy do anything believe in stop resolve	(about)	my his her our their	marriage job relationships studies work life etc

If you take the question given to you by the Querent, and use one of these three formulae, you can, by striking out the inappropriate words, resolve well over 95% of all questions into a straightforward request which has, potentially, a straightforward answer. To go back to our gardening problem, all questions about the fruit resolve themselves into:

a. How must I go about changing my garden, or what must I do to change my garden?
b. Should I change my garden?
c. Will I ever succeed in changing my garden?

These are the archetypal questions; they are never trivial, since ultimately all food comes from some garden or other (try seeing the planet Earth as a garden), and similarly, this world is made up of the conscious and subconscious minds of all its inhabitants.

To finish this chapter, and this section, here is a game that you can play. It is based on a quiz game that was very popular on the radio; to my surprise, many adults to whom I described this game had never heard of it, so I'll first describe the original game (which you can ignore if you know it already) and then the special version for this book.

TWENTY QUESTIONS (i)

A group of people, from three to ten or so, can play. One person is elected who thinks of an *object* (no abstract qualities or ideas) but does not tell any other member of the group. All the other members are allowed to ask questions about the nature of this object, the only proviso being that the person who chose the object can only say 'Yes' or 'No'. You can for instance ask him whether the object is coloured blue, but you cannot ask him what colour the object is. Each member of the group takes it in turn to ask one question. A total of twenty questions only (hence the name) is permitted; by that time the object should have been guessed.

If you didn't succeed the first time, and you have decided that it is a very hard game, try thinking about the following. If you were to make a list of *all* objects and their names that exist in the English language and put them in a special object dictionary, then you could hand over the dictionary to our clever friend, and ask him 'Is the object one of the words in the first half of the dictionary?'; if he said yes, it would be so, if no, then you know it is in the second half. You could then ask him if it was in the last quarter, or the third eighth, or if it is any word between 'prong' or 'pupa', and so on. Mathematically, you can, using twenty questions, ascertain, without any guessing whatsoever, over 1,000,000 words! So, if you didn't succeed the first time, try harder.

TWENTY QUESTIONS (ii)

In the Tarot version of the game, one person is chosen, who must think of a person with whom he has a strong emotional relationship. It can be a parent, a wife or a child; it can be an enemy or a friend, as long as the bond is strong. If the bond is complex, or involves hate or fear, so much the better, since these will show up better in the game.

The chosen person will write about the relationship, but not show it to anyone. He will then tell the other members of the group the way in which he is related, i.e. a father, daughter, friend, enemy, etc.

The rest of the group now ask twenty questions, one each in turn, about the relationship; again, all questions can only be answered 'Yes' or 'No'. After the twenty questions are asked, and the answers noted down, each member of the group then writes down their idea of the exact nature of the relationship, using only one sentence or so. The answers of each member are then read out, and commented on by the person whose relationship is the object of all the attention. This will obviously lead to some discussion.

Finally, in order to demonstrate that all the ideas have been correctly translated, each member of the group is asked to write down a simple action which the person could perform, both physically and mentally, which would or could reverse the relationship.

Here I come to the end of this chapter, and this section. A lot of it is not immediately or directly applicable to learning how to use the Tarot; all of it is knowledge and understanding which I have found necessary for myself as I studied the Tarot. If you don't find an immediate need for it, keep it until you are further on the path, when you may well be better able to make use of it.

part five

Chapter 17

THE NEED FOR PRESENTATION

It is four o'clock in the office and everyone is dreaming over their desks, when gradually the peace is disturbed by one of the cleaners coming round to sell tickets for the Christmas draw in aid of the Fund for Inebriated Washerwomen. She comes to you and suggests you buy two, three, perhaps go wild and buy five. As you hesitate at this totally irrational way of looking at things, at throwing money away, she looks at you with her shrewd eyes out of a lined but experienced face, and says: 'Go on, it's only money; be a devil for once in your life. It'll do you good.' So, reluctantly, you buy.

A few days later, you take the morning off for an important appointment. You have made the important appointment four months earlier by phoning the great man's appointments secretary, and even that was only possible by mentioning the name of a mutual aquaintance, whose letter of introduction you carry with you. You reach his office, which is part of an enormous organization in a fifteen-storey building with millions of pounds worth of equipment, and more than two thousand fellow workers. You announce your direction to the main receptionist, who directs you to the eighth floor where another receptionist asks you to sit down and wait for a few minutes. Your appointment is checked and confirmed, files are opened on your behalf; you sit waiting while telephones ring, intercoms buzz, porters and messengers scurry about. Then at last the great man is ready; you enter his office and there he sits behind an enormous desk with no telephone whatsoever. You are invited to sit down and explain your problems while he listens attentively; after all, that is his job. He doesn't say anything except to prompt you to continue, and it may be months before his opinions as to the solution to your problem are filtered through to you, but the notes on his file will say succinctly 'anal retention'.

Essentially, the cleaner woman and the psychiatrist have come to the same conclusion. They have probably both the same insight into us crazy humans. But which one would you rather accept and believe? Perhaps you are very liberated and really believe that you would take every person at their real value; maybe *you* would, but most people don't. If you were quite honest with yourself you would realize that you wouldn't really accept everyone equally readily. So what is it that makes us accept the words of a shrink and not those of a cleaner?

Well, a shrink is trained, he has had many years of experience at school. But has he? For a start, most of those years were spent training to be a doctor of medicine, mostly physical medicine; after years of very hard work, during which time the student didn't have time to find out what life was about, he then studied three or four more years to finish as a psychiatrist. At no time does he experience life in the way that most of his future patients will experience it. He hasn't done time on an assembly belt, he hasn't been on the dole, he hasn't been bored out of his mind in a dead-end office job. Above all, he hasn't had time to simply sit down with people, friends and aquaintances and simply talk about problems, aspirations, and just everyday things. There simply hasn't been time to do all those things, and there usually never will be in the life of an average doctor or psychiatrist. But the office cleaner has done all these things; in addition, anyone who survives a lifetime at the bottom end of the hierarchy and keeps their good humour picks up enough working knowledge to deal with your average depressed or frustrated office worker. Yet we need psychiatrists in ever increasing numbers, not for the mad, the really mad, but just for the depressed and the frustrated. Why not use cleaners?

Basically, it is very much a matter of presentation. The great man in his office says nothing very much, just murmurs encouragement for you to go on, makes notes and gradually channels you to look at yourself. How do you know that it isn't his secretary occupying the bosses' chair for the day? Would it matter? Most countries have a story about a preacher, a rabbi or a lecturer on tour which goes like this:

> The Great Man is on tour; he rides from town to town in his comfortable limousine, making notes in the back while his chauffeur drives him to the next town. In the evening, they reach the town where he will hold his meeting; the Great Man is wined and dined, while the chauffeur gets shown the servant's quarters. One day the chauffeur suggests to the Great Man that they swap places; the chauffeur knows all the lectures by heart, and would just like to be admired. The Great Man agrees, and at the next town the chauffeur gets the VIP treatment; the next morning he gives the lecture. After the lecture there are questions, and besides the serious questions which just demand common sense and a good memory as to what the Great Man said to a similar question, there are also a few trick questions put by a young man trying to catch out the Great Man. The real Great Man laughs at the chauffeur's predicament; the chauffeur deals with the situation by sneering at the clever young man's ingenuity and suggesting that his 'clever' question is in fact so simple that even his chauffeur could answer it, and here he points to the real Great Man, who is dressed as the chauffeur.

Obviously, for the real difficult cases we need the experienced trained expert; but for the average run-of-the-mill ones the cleaner will do just as well; and there are far more cleaners than psychiatrists.

How does this apply to the Tarot? Well, somehow we must learn to create a feeling of awe and respect. We can't borrow a multi-million pound hospital and all the trappings of equipment and personnel that go with it. We must learn to do with what is at hand. Remember, it is necessary to gain the Querent's respect for the Tarot in order that what is revealed is not wasted. Only by making the Querent feel the same respect and awe that he assigns to consultant psychiatrists are we able to help him.

That is the real meaning of all the hocus-pocus you will hear about the ritual of the cards. Like all of what is called 'magic' there are strong, sensible reasons behind the apparent mystery; it is through the use of these underlying psychological rules in an intelligent fashion that we can make the fullest use of the Tarot.

Chapter 18

TECHNIQUES OF PRESENTATION

The first matter to discuss concerns the storage of your cards. Contrary to what books and practitioners say, the exact manner of storage does not matter in itself. But the care and concern shown by adhering to a given method does. So whether they get stored in a sandalwood box perfumed with incense, or wrapped in a black silk cloth; whether they are stored in a random order, or stored separated into Major and Minor, suits and numerical order; aligned East and West, or vertical, none of these matter in themselves. What does matter is that they are stored in such a way that they are seen to be important. Obviously the Querent must see and be made to notice that you store your cards reverently and in a special way. Subconsciously, you yourself must be aware that the cards are really to be treated with respect. So pick something special, something difficult or expensive to obtain, and then always use it. You must take pains to make the Querent notice it; if you store the cards in a box or silk scarf, always take the box or cloth to the table, complete with the cards, and unwrap them slowly. If the box or the scarf is something outstanding, the Querent notices it, and you can mention the fact that the box has been in the family three generations, or that the scarf is raw silk from the deathbed of a Buddhist monk, or some such.

You yourself must wear something special. Perhaps you have a special dressing gown, or a scarf over your head; a special set of beads, or an armband. It must be noticeable, not to say obtrusive, and again you wear it with the intention of creating a feeling that this garment or whatever is only worn because the cards are special. In real life, how often does the mere putting on of party clothes create a feeling of gaiety within us; the wearing of fancy dress bring out an unsuspected acting talent. Perhaps the special piece of clothing or jewellery can be stored in a special box, which again is brought to the table before being opened.

The cards are unwrapped and laid on the table. The table should be covered with a plain table cloth, of one colour. Patterns in the cloth tend to confuse the spread; a white or black cloth is best, since it provides a good contrast. If you can find something that has a slightly rough surface, such as wool or velvet, it will help in keeping the cards in place once spread, and also in the shuffling if the cards are 'washed'. A cloth used only for laying the cards is a good investment, and can be kept in the same box with the special clothing.

Lighting is very important. The actual level of lighting is not as important as the absence of glare; neither the Querent nor the Reader should have to squint in glare. Glare can be caused by a bright window in an otherwise dark room, a strong unshaded light such as a bare bulb near the ceiling; if you cannot switch off the naked light, just make sure that neither Reader nor Querent has to look into the light. A good atmosphere can be created by drawing the curtains, and switching on a table lamp to one side, placed between Querent and Reader. Perhaps a candle in a special candlestick, or an oil-lamp if you can get hold of one. Anything that will shine a soft friendly light on both people. It is just as important that the Querent can see and trust the Reader, as the other way round. Being mystical and mysterious won't help in building up trust.

Next comes a cup of tea. Oh yes, it really does. First of all, tea, or coffee for that matter, contains caffeine; this is a drug which can be used to speed up your synapses, to raise your sensitivity to very small signals. Most people drink tea or coffee out of habit whenever they want something hot, or they are thirsty. Habitual users of tea and coffee won't notice the effects of the drug, they are permanently 'high', and in fact live in a state of continual irritation, or alternatively, they learn to tune their body in such a way that there is less sensitivity. In both cases the extra sensitivity obtained through use of caffeine is lost. But if you drink tea or coffee sparingly, or not at all, and then drink a strong cup of either, the effect is noticeable, and will help you in your reading. That is the practical use of coffee. But the drink will also help in setting the presentation. It will create a sense of ritual, it will enable you to share 'bread and salt', and it will help you in 'observing' the Querent.

'Observing' the Querent is a very important part of the whole reading. To understand what that means, we must go back to Sherlock Holmes and his flat in Baker Street. When the door is opened to his study, and a new client walks in, Holmes will remark casually to the astonished Watson that the visitor is obviously an undertaker, belongs to the Rotary, is left-handed, practises photography as a hobby, plays guitar, has been recently widowed and has an eighteen-year old daughter with blonde hair. Sherlock Holmes 'observed' at a conscious level, with great speed and accuracy, and used the information so gained to come to conclusions concerning the case.

The Reader in a Tarot reading will be doing the same, but letting his subconscious do the work. Obviously, the subconscious needs a little time, and a range of actions on the part of the Querent so as to gather some facts. It is very important when observing is done that it be done with the subconscious, and not with the conscious. The conscious will see that the Querent is foreign, is poor and perhaps uneducated in the niceties of English grammar and accent. The conscious will then say, 'Aha, I must be extra nice (or careful, or suspicious) because the person is poor, is foreign, is uneducated, or whatever'. Both positive and negative prejudices influence the quality and accuracy of a reading. Let the subconscious observe that the person is honest, intelligent and sensitive, none of which qualities conflict with those noticed by the conscious, but do give us an entirely different picture.

'Observing' can be done by sharing a cup of tea with the Querent, and by talking with them about casual matters. While drinking the cup of tea, we can talk about the weather, the locality in which the Querent lives, what they think about transport to this place, and so on. Their microscopically small reactions to the words you use act almost as a word-association test as used by the psychoanalysts. Your conscious won't notice the Querent's reactions, but your subconscious will.

At this stage, if you like the smell, you can light some incense. It is pretty to watch the vapour trails, masks homely smells such as cooking and unwashed feet, and again creates atmosphere. You may also wish to wash your hands at this stage, after having drunk the tea and lit the incense; ritual purification increases the sense of awe and respect held with regard to the special feeling of an object.

Now we come to the shuffling of the cards. The actual shuffling is not very important, but the effect that it can create is. There are two main methods; the first one is usually called 'washing' and consists of laying the cards face down on the table and using both hands; push the cards at random across the table and across each other. This is where the slightly rough table cloth helps. The cards are swirled slowly around; perhaps the Querent is allowed to help. Then the cards are picked up as a disorganized bundle and stacked into a nice flat pack once more.

The second method consists of taking the whole pack in the left hand, and using the thumb and two fingers of the right hand as a sort of pincers, pick up part of the pack with the right hand. The cards are picked up and lifted just high enough to lift over the remainder of the pack still left in the left hand, and dropped into the left hand, in front of the pack. This action is repeated again and again, so as to shuffle the whole pack thoroughly. The action should be slow, and hypnotic; while it is going on, the Reader continues to talk with the Querent. But now the talk is about the question that is going to be asked.

When the cards have been shuffled to your satisfaction (this point will have been reached when both the Reader and Querent feel they are 'connecting'), they are spread out flat onto the table, and the Querent is asked to choose the required number of cards. The cards are picked up, one at a time, without looking at the face of the card, till the number required for any given spread has been reached. Incidentally, the hand movements and the order in which the cards are picked will enable the observant Reader to gain a lot of insight into the character of the Querent.

How to ask the question, and how to direct the Querent into asking the proper question have already been dealt with elsewhere. There is still one major item in the presentation that requires discussion, and that is the matter of payment. I will leave that for the next chapter.

Chapter 19

PAYMENT AND SACRIFICE

We, the willing, are led by the unknowing to do the impossible, for the ungrateful. We've done so much with so little for so long we're now totally qualified to do anything with nothing.

(small notice seen in several builder's shops)

All the most successful psychiatrists in America agree that charging the patient a high fee has a strong therapeutic effect.

Here are two comments, from the despairing to the cynical, about an attitude people have to receiving and giving. And there are you, dear reader, faced with a Querent whose cards you're about to read. The time has come to cross your palm with silver. From alternative flower-children to nice old ladies retired in Palm Springs, from London secretaries doing it for their friends to earnest amateur psychiatrists only trying to help their friends, I hear a united cry 'How horrid!'; I have visions of a vast horde of people gathered in the street outside my publisher with placards denouncing me for my greedy capitalist ideas.

Hold it, let me tell you a little about people. This whole area is like a minefield, with every step bringing you the possibility of setting off a highly explosive bomb. I think it will be necessary to go slowly and, like a bomb disposal expert, defuse every mine.

First of all, the value that people set on anything depends on what they must sacrifice in order to obtain it. Many people in my family have been artists, and so gradually over the years we have collected paintings by members of the family and by friends whose paintings we have bought or been given as presents. The paintings just hang on the walls because we like them; sometimes we have more paintings than we know what to do with. We hang them in the hall, the bathroom (honest) and the spare bedroom. Till one day we realize that all those paintings done by one's great-uncle are now famous and much sought-after works; the member of the family lent, sold and gave the works to the nation. It's a shock to realize that the painting of flowers is by Vincent van Gogh, or the charming portrait is by Mondrian; they suddenly become too valuable to be hung in the bathroom or the hall. We have to insure them, hang them in good light, have strangers traipse round the house in their pursuit of Art; their equivalent of a century ago would never have given these paintings more than a few seconds scrutiny. Their value is changed because the sacrifice which people will make in order to acquire, or even see, these paintings has changed; the paintings themselves have not changed in any way.

Similarly, a friend of mine had, hanging proudly in his living room, a signed and numbered print of Picasso; to me it looked a quick dash of the pen, something quite interesting but no more interesting than some of the work of my five-year old niece. I hasten to add that I like both their works. One day my friend found out the print was a forgery; instantly the piece was banished to the dark part of the hall. Why was the piece suddenly worth so much less?

The advice and insight a Reader can offer depends very much on the sacrifice a Querent has to make. In an earlier chapter we saw the difference between a man receiving advice from his tealady and from an eminent psychiatrist. Now think how many more sacrifices, in time and money, the man has to make to see the psychiatrist. Very few people will sneer at an expensive painting; the scoffers rarely turn down the opportunity of having such a costly painting gracing their home. Psychologically, it becomes very hard to ignore advice from a man who charges $40 an hour; you will have to think deep and hard before you do so. It is just this, the idea of forcing people to *think*, that is the real service a Tarot reader can perform for the Querent. It is for this reason that payment for reading the Tarot is not an unnecessary evil, but a positive part of the service.

The second reason why such a payment is required has to do with the relationship between the Reader and Querent. In our lives we make a distinction between two types of transaction. The first type is when we have to give something to another, or receive something from another. The second type is when we pay our way, and either give, or receive, value for money.

When we have either to give or receive, we make a transaction of a very dishonest nature. The giver can feel superior, since he has been noble, kind, and good; the receiver has to feel humble, and grateful, and render thanks. One of the marks of the superior man is his ability to give without making the recipient feel inferior, and his ability to receive gifts without making himself feel humble. Most of us are just ordinary slobs who go through this identifying of role every time we receive or give.

All of us have grown up in cultures where we are told, 'It is greater to give than to receive', or some such equivalent. We are impure little beings, so we tend to be selfish and want to own everything. Yet our parents and teachers enjoin on us to give, give, give till it hurts. We grow up to feel, every time we give, both pride and pleasure in overcoming our ancient selves. We feel guilty, each time we receive, that we have given in to our ancient sin of wanting everything. That is why in groups and societies devoted to developing the psyche, one of the most prevalent types is the person who wants to give; they are the most irritating, since they don't know how to receive.

John Steinbeck, in his books about the waterfront and the bums who lived there, books like *Cannery Row* and *Sweet Thursday*, made the point that 'it is greater to receive than to give' since it demands a much more developed person in order to receive graciously. Until both Querent and Reader can give and receive, the contra-flow of emotions from recipient to giver will often cause all manner of unhealthy emotions. These can be easily avoided by allowing the Querent to pay. Firstly the Querent can then feel he has in turn given something to the Reader, thus cancelling the transaction. Secondly, the Querent can then feel that he is being treated as an adult, who has paid his own way, rather than as a child who is dependant on the unpredictable goodness of grown-ups.

The last major reason concerns only full-time Tarot readers. Such a person needs to live; if you agree, with Johnson, that you fail to see the necessity, then obviously you don't seek to make use of the services of the Tarot. But others do, and in order to make such services easily available, there is room for full-time readers. Very often, if you meet a famous guru, you do not pay for this privilege;

others, his immediate followers or members of his congregation, do. If you consult a psychiatrist on Medicare, you do not pay him at the time, but you will have paid taxes, or other people will have paid them. If the Reader of the Tarot came to your house, and stayed the night and ate with you, you would have provided his necessities; the cost of food and space would be greater than the cost of a reading, yet it is 'invisible.' For a guru to trust in God, and live all his life on the generosity of people who recognize his genius, is not easily possible in our Western society. 'Render unto Caesar what is Caesar's', then you can afford to 'render unto God what is God's.'

You may object, after all this, that you don't need the money; if that is really so, you can give it to charity, since the poor are always with us. But don't tell the Querent; it is none of his business to know what happens to the money, and probably your only reason for telling him the money is going to charity is to try to look less rapacious and more noble in his eyes.

The matter of payment should be brought up openly and directly. A statement such as 'I always charge $10.00 (or whatever)' when people ask you if you can read their Tarot will stop idle curiosity and encourage people with real problems. Real problems are problems which would be worth $10.00 to find an answer. You can then add, 'In your case I will reduce it because I can see that you cannot easly afford it, but I can see that you really need it.'

If people complain that this is far too much, ask them how much they paid last time they saw a hairdresser, or what is the price of seeing a good film followed by coffee and cake. Especially if people complain of the high price, do not lower it. It is almost always a particularly unpleasant trait in their character to always 'price' everything, including friendship, loyalty and honesty, and then try to bargain down to a market-stall price. The best treatment for meanness is to charge more.

I think that it is by now quite obvious that what I have talked about as 'payment' is really 'sacrifice'. Once you see it in that light, then the whole thing changes, and we can examine the problem in a much more elevated manner. Incidently, the priests in the olden days always received their share of the sacrifice for personal living expenses; priests also need to live.

How much to charge in order to make the contribution a 'sacrifice' and not just an expense is a matter for the intuitive insight of the Reader. Obviously, the same fee, which is a prohibitive amount for an under-paid student nurse, is small change to the idle wife of a rich company director. Following an ancient religious practice, I find that a fee representing about 10% of their income after taxes is about the right balance. If you generally charge a reading fee of 10% of the average (median) income of the country you live in, then you can reduce it as you see fit. Raising it is more difficult, and in order to force the very rich to make an appropriate sacrifice calls for ingenuity.

One way out is to realize that a sacrifice can be made using other media than money. For a rich businessman, it can be time, for an idle person it can mean some physical task; for a vain person it can mean looking less beautiful; for some people it can mean a refusal to be paid.

Usually the businessman is short of time; then he must sacrifice time. Charge him your standard fee, but insist that your only free time is on Monday morning; that is a real sacrifice. Perhaps you haven't time yourself during the day. Fine, then you can ask him to pick up, personally, an article from an occult shop that you have ordered by phone. Check afterwards that he picked it up himself, and didn't send his secretary.

An idle person should be given an appointment before eight in the morning, or be told that until you have finished the task of folding five thousand business letters you can't begin to read, and could he give a hand meanwhile.

Sometimes the shock of not being able to pay their way, but having to receive something for nothing can act in a positive way with people. The sacrifice should be tailored to the individual, so that in following the task, part of the 'cure' advised during the reading is undertaken. But it shouldn't be made blatant. Instead, at some time after the reading and during the subsequent conversation the idea should be introduced that if sacrifice isn't made, then their subconscious will feel too ill at ease to make full use of the advice offered during the reading. All the Querent's efforts will be in vain; in other words, there is no sneaky way of obtaining the advice at a cut rate. It is almost like buying a cheap book guaranteeing to make you rich. It is written in Russian, and by the time you can read enough Russian to understand the book, you can make a good living as a translator.

I shall end this chapter by telling the story of the Prince who fell ill. He had a charming wife, was head of a rich country, there were no enemies, and his people loved him. However, he fell ill, not badly enough to die, but he was unhealthy enough so as to make life miserable. No doctor seemed able to cure him, and many tried, but in vain. One day, a strange doctor came, who offered to cure him. The treatment was to consist of a secret salve which was contained in the handles of two wooden clubs. The Prince was to swing the clubs twice a day for half-an-hour; as he swung them the salve would penetrate his skin and eventually cure him. Sure enough, after three months, the Prince became better. Only then would the strange doctor reveal the secret of his cure. 'Exercise,' he said, 'That's all you needed. You wouldn't have believed me if I had told you then. Now just make sure you get some every day.'

Please, just try to be a little imaginative in your sacrifices. A sense of humour helps.

Chapter 20

THE CONTRACT

The last subject to be discussed is the Contract between Reader and Querent. Contracts are agreements between consenting and willing individuals whereby party A agrees to provide goods or a service to B in consideration of a return based on goods or services. Both parties promise something, and both have to be satisfied before the contract is completed. Contracts can be written or spoken – complicated, written, signed and sealed documents, as well as unspoken, everyday arrangements.

For instance, there is no written arrangement that after I have eaten a meal at a friend's house I will help with the washing up; if I don't nobody will say anything, but eventually, if I continue to eat my fill while watching other people do the work, our friendship will suffer, and be wound up. Yet we have never discussed the matter, whilst the idea of a written agreement seems ludicrous.

At the other end, when I wear my hat labelled 'architect' I have to administer very complicated contracts. Sometimes these contracts are worth millions of pounds; they run for pages and pages, and refer to drawings, and schedules and specifications. Shortly after I left my architectural school, I worked for an architect who expected all builders to be 'thieves, rogues and vagebonds'. I worked there for about a year, and during that period I had to deal with several firms of builders who used to make a lot of trouble. One of them used to write a letter each and every day claiming that a certain item was not in the contract, and that therefore it would have to be an extra. To prove that it was in the contract might take several hours of laborious research, for which there was no extra payment. Obviously, if the builder hired an extra man at, say £3,000 a year to find loop-holes, then by working at nothing else, he would easily earn his pay several times over.

I tell this story to show that there is no contract that is completely water-tight. All contracts demand good will on both sides. My boss had a bad attitude to builders, and he certainly received confirmation of his suspicions. I personally have had very little trouble with builders, but then perhaps I like working with my hands, and I like and respect other people who do.

The previous chapter was about what contribution the Querent must make; obviously he is making a contribution in the expectation that he will gain something in return. This forms the basis of the Contract between Querent and Reader.

The Contract is not written, not spoken, not even alluded to. The Querent will even, usually, be unable to think about it; but there will be a vague hope for decent treatment. It is therefore necessary for the Reader to imagine, control and enforce this mystical Contract. The best analogy I can think of is the situation when the nearest member of the family has to arrange the funeral of the dear departed. Very few of us know anything very much about what we should do in such a situation, or how we should behave; the undertaker is there not only to arrange practical matters, but also to subtly guide you through all the proper expressions of grief. Do not, obviously, see a reading as a funeral, but just try to guide the Querent through the actions which will produce the best results. We have already seen some of this guidance when I was discussing 'presentation' and 'payment'.

One of the most important guidelines in the Contract is that the Reader be honest. I can almost feel your instant reaction to this requirement; of course you are honest, nobody doubted you for one minute. But there is a special way of being honest. In reading spreads, you will start droning out your feelings, and gradually you stray away from talking about the cards and their meanings, and into an area where you may feel you are just spouting forth opinions prejudices and stray thoughts. The temptation here is to either withhold these unlikely ideas, or to dress them up in somewhat more logical terms. Don't. Be honest, and just talk the words as the cards fall. These ideas are precisely the ones which can be generated only by the Tarot or similar 'psychic mirrors'; they are the most valuable thoughts.

Often people will object to total honesty on the grounds that it surely can't be right to talk about someone's death or other unpleasant things they can foresee, nor would they like to tell the Querent unpleasant things about their character. The counter-argument is that in the first place the Tarot not only allows you to see things that otherwise would be hidden, it will also show you the best way to inform the Querent so as to *communicate* this informa-tion. The Tarot is a selective mirror which does not show you all the things going on in your subconscious; it only illuminates the answer to the question.

Also remember that people only hear and notice things that they want to know. The information they want to know is already in their subconscious; when you read the Tarot, you are merely transferring information from the Querent's subconscious to his conscious. If they *still* don't want to know, their subconscious will again suppress it. Often, when the family doctor has to break the news to a patient that he is doomed to die within six months, the patient will tell the doctor he has known for the last year, and has made all his arrange-ments on the assumption. Then again, other patients will not hear or believe such a prediction; however often you tell them, they do not notice it. The dangers of car-driving or cigarette-smoking are very well-known, yet people, including myself, indulge in such danger-ous activities. How can you tell somebody something if they don't want to know? For this reason, you can be as honest as you like, without ever worrying about the consequences.

Lastly, the Reader's duty in fulfilling the Contract is to try to re-educate the Querent. As I have said, the Querent's subconscious already knew the answer. The inability to transfer such knowledge from subconscious to conscious in the mind of the Querent is caused by various fears (angst in the psychology/psychotherapy language); we can lessen this fear by discussion after the reading, and during the reading we can talk about some of the deeper symbolism of the cards in the Tarot; as I have said each reading can be a miniature lecture on some of the aspects of the study of the Tarot.

Here I will leave you in your study of the Tarot. Your study has begun; mine has been helped a little on the way by the need to order my thoughts. Beyond a certain stage there seems to be no real teacher; the teacher is taught how and what to teach by teaching the student. Somewhere a synergetic principle is involved, which includes the teacher, the student, the world and the subject being discussed.

part six

Chapter 21

POST SCRIPTUM

'I was a Moron till I became an Idiot; now I am studying hard to become a Fool'.*

Moron, mor'on, mör'on, n. a somewhat feeble-minded person, one who remains at the mental age of eight to twelve throughout life. (Greek mŏros, foolish)
Idiot, id'i-ət, id'yət, n. one inflicted with the severest grade of feeblemindedness, a foolish or unwise person. (Greek idiŏtēs, a private person, ordinary person, one who holds no public office or has no professional knowledge)
Fool, fŏol, n. one wanting in wisdom, judgement or sense, a Jester.

We are all Morons to begin with; we follow the dictates of the world and grub around trying to fit in with the order of things. Sometimes we rebel and become alternative and groovy; but it is still conformity to a standard set up by the people around.The business man with hand-cut suit, smart tie and linen shirt cannot wear sandals; the busker in the Underground tunnel who wears jeans, old shirt with Levi jacket and wears a 'short-back-and-sides' haircut, and gets jeered at by his peer-group. The business man cannot take the afternoon off to sunbathe on a Tuesday, just because the weather is beautiful. Nor could an 'alternative' guy be too proud of his regular job; there would be mutterings of 'protestant work ethic'. The main thing all Morons have in common is the desperate insistence on the 'rightness' of certain principles, whether they be 'motherhood', 'honesty', 'keeping cool', 'property is theft', etc. They may disagree on any number of points with the rest of society, they may feel unsure of much, including themselves, but they identify with a programme of ideas and feelings that are

Tarot Therapy was originally published in Great Britain under the title *Tarot-mania, or why only an Idiot would want to become a fool.*

common to all their set. Sooner or later in any discussion you will hear the expression: 'Surely you agree that . . .' It is the stage that young people go through, when they know it all so much better than their elders, when they discover their parent's clay feet, and also know that they are never going to get caught. The Moron stays stuck in this stage.

When the Moron feels so unsure of himself that he cannot or will not say or think any more that some things are 'right', then he becomes an Idiot. Looked at another way, he is sure enough of himself to admit to himself that he doesn't know; he likes himself enough not to worry that other people won't approve any more just because he cannot assert himself. The Greek word 'idiotes' referred to someone who didn't know, and *knew* that he didn't know, because it was not his business to know. He was not an official, or a professional, and therefore held no public liability for his opinions. His ideas, facts and judgements were only opinions, and everybody valued them as such.

Only when you admit your ignorance does it become possible to learn from someone who *does* know. In purely practical terms I have found it easier to teach shop assistants and factory hands outside London, than to teach the *Time Out* kids who had already dabbled for years in astrology, gestalt therapy and bio-energy.

Finally the Moron, through constant realization of his lack of knowledge, till this awareness runs through all thoughts and actions, begins to realize that other people, including his teacher and all the wise men that ever lived, don't know it either. If the Moron can accept that, and laugh at the preposterous pretentiousness of the Universe, why, he has become a Fool. Because he is not caught up with the need to justify his actions and ideas in terms of the opinion of other people (in modern terms, he is self-directed), he can do or say totally foolish things, which may well be the most relevant and apposite. Just like the Jester in a Mediaeval Court, whose antics were but a vehicle for transcendant insight. In the Tarot, the Fool is the first and last card, it is the card without number. The Fool can do anything, be anything, say anything. In a sense, the Fool is the person who allows the Will of God to flow through without impedance.

The change from being a Moron to becoming an Idiot is a matter of insight into one's situation, and the use of some will-power to get out of it. Often the change is initiated by a shock, a disruption to one's comfortable environment. But the change from Idiot to Fool requires tremendous work on oneself; the use of the Tarot is one way to aid the work.

RECOMMENDED READING

(Publisher's Note: The original British edition of this book contained a bibliography citing a number of works that were available only in the United Kingdom. Following is a list of books currently available in the United States, contributed by three of the foremost experts in the field: Eileen Connolly, Mary K. Greer, and Gail Fairfield.)

Arrien, Angeles. *The Tarot Workbook*. Sonoma, Ca.: Arcus, 1984.

Butler, Bill. *Dictionary of the Tarot*. New York: Schocken, 1975.

Case, Paul Foster. *The Tarot: A Key to the Wisdom of the Ages*. Richmond, Va.: Macoy, 1974.

Connolly, Eileen. *Tarot: The Handbook for the Apprentice*. North Hollywood, Ca.: Newcastle, 1984.

———. *Tarot: The Handbook for the Journeyman*. North Hollywood, Ca.: Newcastle, 1987.

Douglas, Alfred. *The Tarot: The Origins, Meanings and Uses of the Cards*. Baltimore: Penguin, 1973.

Fairfield, Gail. *Choice-Centered Tarot*. North Hollywood, Ca.: Newcastle, 1984.

Gearhart, Sally. *A Feminist Tarot: A Guide to Intrapersonal Communication*. New York: Persephone, 1977.

Gray, Eden. *Mastering the Tarot*. New York: New American Library, 1971.

Greer, Mary K. *Tarot Constellations: Patterns of Personal Destiny*. North Hollywood, Ca.: Newcastle, 1987.

———. *Tarot for Your Self: A Workbook for Personal Transformation*. North Hollywood, Ca.: Newcastle, 1984.

Noble, Vicki. *Motherpiece: A Way to the Goddess Through Myth, Art and Tarot*. San Francisco: Harper & Row, 1983.

Pollack, Rachel. *Seventy-Eight Degrees of Wisdom: A Book of Tarot*. Wellingborough, Northamptonshire: Aquarian Press, 1980.

Potts, Billie. *A New Women's Tarot*. Woodstock: Elf and Dragon's Press, 1978.

(The following works, which relate to symbols, divination, and esoteric studies, appeared in the author's original bibliography and are available in the United States.)

Berne, Eric. *Games People Play*. New York: Ballantine, 1978.

Graves, Robert. *The White Goddess*. New York: Peter Smith, 1983.

Gurdjieff, G. I. *Meetings with Remarkable Men*. New York: Dutton, 1969.

Ouspensky, P. D. *In Search of the Miraculous: Fragments of an Unknown Teaching*. New York: Harcourt, 1965.

Pierce, J. R. *An Introduction to Information Theory: Symbols, Signals & Noise*. New York: Dover, 1980.

Shah, Idries. *The Subtleties of the Inimitable Mulla Nasrudin*. New York: Institute for the Study of Human Knowledge, 1983.

———. *The Sufis*. New York: Institute for the Study of Human Knowledge, 1983.